# Oda Nobunaga

Samurai Commander 1534–82

Stephen Turnbull

Helion & Company Limited
Unit 8 Amherst Business Centre
Budbrooke Road
Warwick
CV34 5WE
England
Tel. 01926 499 619
Email: info@helion.co.uk
Website: www.helion.co.uk
X (formerly Twitter): @Helionbooks
Facebook: @HelionBooks
Visit our blog https:// helionbooks.wordpress.com/

Published by Helion & Company 2025
Designed and typeset by Mary Woolley, Battlefield Design (www.battlefield-design.co.uk)
Cover designed by Paul Hewitt, Battlefield Design (www.battlefield-design.co.uk)

Text © Stephen Turnbull 2025
Illustrations from Author's collection unless otherwise stated
Front cover artwork by and © Emmanuel Valerio 2025
Maps by Mark Thompson © Helion & Company 2025

Every reasonable effort has been made to trace copyright holders and to obtain their permission for the use of copyright material. The author and publisher apologise for any errors or omissions in this work and would be grateful if notified of any corrections that should be incorporated in future reprints or editions of this book.

ISBN 978-1-804518-36-6

British Library Cataloguing-in-Publication Data.
A catalogue record for this book is available from the British Library.

All rights reserved. No part of this publication may be reproduced, stored in a retrieval system, or transmitted, in any form, or by any means, electronic, mechanical, photocopying, recording or otherwise, without the express written consent of Helion & Company Limited.

For details of other military history titles published by Helion & Company Limited contact the above address or visit our website: http://www.helion.co.uk.

We always welcome receiving book proposals from prospective authors.

# Contents

| | | |
|---|---|---|
| Dedication | | iv |
| Introduction: The Enigma Who Was Oda Nobunaga | | v |
| 1 | The Ruthless Fool | 9 |
| 2 | The Road to Okehazama | 27 |
| 3 | Nobunaga and the Shogun | 36 |
| 4 | Nobunaga and the Battle of Anegawa | 47 |
| 5 | Nobunaga and the Ikkō Ikki | 63 |
| 6 | Nobunaga Triumphant | 77 |
| 7 | From Nagashima to Nagashino | 84 |
| 8 | Bullets and Battleships | 99 |
| 9 | The Final Years | 113 |
| Colour Plates Commentary | | 126 |
| Bibliography | | 128 |

# Dedication

To Marlene.

# Introduction

# The Enigma Who Was Oda Nobunaga

At first, there had been nothing unusual about the grand New Year's banquet held at Gifu castle on the first day of the first month of the Second Year of Tenshō, a date that corresponds to 23 January 1574 on the western calendar. Its genial host was the daimyo (literally 'big name' or warlord) Oda Nobunaga (1534–1582). He had much to celebrate, because the First Year of Tenshō had been a very good year indeed. With his followers gathered around him, Nobunaga accepted their kind wishes and proposed a toast, at which merry moment the *takokushū* ('outsiders') – in other words, those who had only submitted to Nobunaga's authority after his triumphant march into Japan's capital city of Kyoto in 1568 – were politely excused.

Once they had gone, a second banquet began that was attended only by Nobunaga's closest military associates: his veteran Horse Guards, many of whom had served him loyally since the days when he had been only a minor warlord in a province surrounded by enemies. Nobunaga had much to thank them for, particularly in terms of what they had helped him achieve over the previous few months, so he had prepared a little surprise. As the Horse Guards grew all the more tipsy from the *sake* they were consuming, their eyes were suddenly drawn towards three plain wooden trays that were carried into the hall by servants and placed in front of them. Each tray held a single gold-lacquered human skull.

It is more than likely that the Horse Guards needed no explanation as to whose heads these ghastly trophies had been before their deaths. All three had already been exhibited publicly in Kyoto with the flesh slowly rotting and flies buzzing round them to serve as a reminder to commoners and courtiers alike of the folly of opposing Oda Nobunaga. Their new and aesthetically more pleasing exposure would also have been a poignant reminder to the Horse Guards of their own service to Nobunaga, because all of those present would have participated in at least one of the battles of Anegawa, Odani or Ichijōdani that had led to this hat-trick of noble

# ODA NOBUNAGA: SAMURAI COMMANDER 1534–82

decapitations. At those engagements, the Horse Guards had fought and beaten Asakura Yoshikage (1533–1573), the daimyo of Echizen province, his ally Azai Hisamasa (1524–1573) of Ōmi province and Hisamasa's son and heir, Azai Nagamasa (1545–1573), who just happened to be Oda Nobunaga's own brother-in-law. Their gilded skulls had now become the life and soul of the party.

The Asakura and Azai families had posed serious threats to Nobunaga not only because of their considerable military strength but also because of their close proximity to Nobunaga's sphere of influence. Japan may have boasted many daimyo who were even more powerful than the Asakura and Azai, but those titans ruled from far away and were unlikely to threaten Nobunaga's ambitions for the time being, and his ambitions were huge. The Hōjō of the area of Eastern Japan that now includes modern Tokyo were a case in point. They were all-powerful within their own sphere of influence but posed no threat to Oda Nobunaga until very late in their history. I traced the evolution of the Hōjō clan over five generations in my previous Helion book *Hōjō: Samurai Warlords 1487-1590* and suggested that the whole of Japan's sixteenth-century military revolution could be understood through the history of that one family.[1] In this present book, I will examine the popular notion that a similar journey from retinue to regiment may be traced through the remarkable life of the samurai warlord and national unifier Oda Nobunaga.

Oda Nobunaga, the most controversial leader in samurai history, depicted here seated in his palace dressed as a heroic archer. (ESSK 1803, detail; for a guide to abbreviations, see the Bibliography)

A warrior child of his times (one might even say an infant prodigy), Nobunaga emerged on to the Japanese scene to a background of a country that had been at war with itself for decades. He became Japan's first unifier after many years of civil war and earned immortality by an early death, yet he remains one of the most controversial characters in the whole of Japanese history. Vilified by Sir George Sansom in his *History of Japan* as a 'cruel and callous brute', Nobunaga is still a divisive figure to this day.[2] He achieved results both on the battlefield and off it with a ruthlessness that others feared and few emulated, yet, to his many admirers, he is credited with military innovations ranging from the invention of iron-clad warships to the introduction of controlled volley firing of

---

1  Stephen Turnbull, *Hōjō: Samurai Warlords 1487-1590* (Warwick: Helion and Company, 2023).
2  George Sansom, *A History of Japan, 1334-1615* (London: Cresset Press, 1961), p.310.

muskets. Nobunaga's political achievements are also lauded and include the abolition of the Ashikaga Shogunate after two centuries of power and the establishment of Japan's first cordial relations with Europe. Most important of all, say his supporters, through a series of victories by a loyal and well-organised army, Nobunaga began the process that was eventually to lead to the reunification of Japan under one leader, a goal that only his unexpected and violent death prevented Nobunaga from achieving for himself.

By contrast, his detractors note that Nobunaga's legacy includes some of the cruellest civilian massacres in Japanese history. For example, he destroyed Japan's great seat of learning at the monastery of Enryakuji on Mount Hiei, and, in several other similar operations, he slaughtered thousands of local warriors who had banded together in hostile leagues to oppose him. Even his achievements on the battlefield have been called into question, because modern historical research has criticised the one aspect of his character that for centuries was almost universally accepted: that of being a military genius. This book will tackle this very point, examining Nobunaga's military career in detail and asking in particular if he can be credited in any way with beginning Japan's military revolution.

## Historical Sources for Oda Nobunaga

Good or bad, Oda Nobunaga is a larger-than-life character in Japanese history, so there is no shortage of written material on which to base an assessment of him. He was the first Japanese person to be described by European visitors, and their accounts of him are very revealing. Those authors were, however, Christian missionaries who saw in Nobunaga's antipathy to militant Buddhism a very clear example of the principle that 'my enemy's enemy is my friend'. Their assessment of Nobunaga's callous acts against Buddhist institutions is therefore almost totally positive, as are their enthusiastic descriptions of Nobunaga's victories, his castles and his grand lifestyle.

As for Japanese sources, some lively details of Nobunaga's battles may be found in the chronicle *Mikawa Gofudo ki*, although, when heroics are concerned, its emphasis lies primarily with his lifetime ally Tokugawa Ieyasu (1542–1616).[3] Most important of all, however, is Nobunaga's highly detailed biography *Shinchō-Kō ki* ('The Chronicle of Lord Nobunaga'). It was written by a close follower of his called Ōta Gyūichi, who was an eyewitness to many of the events he describes. Gyūichi celebrates Nobunaga for his military and political genius, and the work is hardly less gushing in its praise than are the panegyrics of the Jesuits. In *Shinchō-Kō ki*, Nobunaga's enemies topple before him partly as a result of his military acumen and partly because of the remorseless workings of the 'Way of Heaven' (*Tendō*),

---

3　Two versions are used here: Narushima Motonao (ed.), *Kaisei Mikawa Gofudo ki* (Tokyo: Kinshōdō, 1886), vol. 1; Kuwata Tadachika and Utagawa Terao (eds), *Kaisei Mikawa Gofudo ki* (Tokyo: Akita Shoten, 1976), vols 1–2.

a grandiose principle of fate that always seems to favour Nobunaga until his final, bitter end.

My translations from *Shinchō-Kō ki* are based mainly on Kuwata's book as referenced below, but I have also made much use of the invaluable 2011 translation into English by Elisonas and Lamers.[4] Not only does their remarkable work provide a thorough compendium of source material, but the authors also dissect Ōta Gyūichi's many shortcomings concerning dates and chronology and identify every location that is mentioned. Their book should also be read in conjunction with Lamers' own biography of Nobunaga, which goes beyond *Shinchō-Kō ki* and incorporates the European material noted above.[5] With two such heavyweight volumes available, it may be thought that nothing else could be added to the mix, but the reader's attention is also directed towards Neil McMullin's book on the Buddhist factions against whom Nobunaga fought for almost a decade.[6]

In the pages that follow, I shall attempt to tell the story of Oda Nobunaga first and foremost as a military man. I will examine critically his prowess on the battlefield, in particular his four famous victories at Okehazama, Anegawa, Nagashino and Kizugawaguchi, and will set them beside a number of other engagements when Nobunaga used acts of civilian massacre as a weapon of warfare. In addition, I shall investigate Nobunaga's place in the development of military technology in Japan. His army organisation and structure will also be examined in detail along with his choice of arms and armour and battlefield heraldry.

As is usual, I present Japanese names with the surname first. In most cases, I have converted lunar calendar dates to western-style ones while retaining some lunar dates for context and effect. To add to the written material consulted here, I have personally visited every battlefield at which Nobunaga fought, every castle that he established and every modern museum and monument dedicated to his memory. I would therefore like to thank the many museum curators and private collectors of prints and illustrated books who allowed me to take the photographs that appear here. These pictures, many of which have never been published before, have allowed me to portray Nobunaga's celebrated generals and armies in realistically imaged action, together with much new information about their flags and heraldry. Once again, Emmanuel Valerio has transformed my ideas into a stunning colour plate and cover picture. I hope that this wide range of illustrative material will complement the text and do justice to the highly challenging character of Oda Nobunaga.

---

4 Kuwata Tadachika (ed.), *Shinchō-Kō ki* (Tokyo: Jinbutsu Ōraisha, 1965); J. S. A. Elisonas and J. P. Lamers (trans and eds), *The Chronicle of Lord Nobunaga by Ōta Gyūichi* (Leiden: Brill, 2011).

5 Jeroen Lamers, *Japonius Tyrannus: The Japanese Warlord Oda Nobunaga Reconsidered* (Leiden: Hotei, 2000).

6 Neil McMullin, *Buddhism and the State in Sixteenth-Century Japan* (Princeton: Princeton University Press, 1984).

# 1

# The Ruthless Fool

It is usually accepted that Oda Nobunaga was born on the twenty-eighth day of the fifth month of the Third Year of Tenbun (9 July 1534) at Shobata castle in Owari province, which is now the western half of modern Aichi Prefecture. His father was the accomplished Oda Nobuhide (1510–1551), a local warrior of great renown yet one whose status was far from that of being either the lord of the whole of Owari or even the head of the entire Oda family, which was grievously split into two branches. Nevertheless, as a collective entity, those who bore the surname of Oda had not only survived the turmoil that had arisen out of the momentous events of the past century but had also done very well out of it. Only their internal divisions now prevented any one of them from ruling Owari in peace, although open armed conflict between the two branches took some years to become established.

The previous hundred years in Japan had been dominated by the famously traumatic Ōnin War, which had begun in 1467 and lasted a decade, leaving Japan so full of new rivalries and conflicts that none could say for sure when it had actually ended.[1] It had, however, become evident to all that the military power of the shogun (the military ruler of Japan under the god-like emperor) had been irredeemably broken, even though his name and charisma remained intact. When they realised that a new impotence now lay at the centre of governance, local leaders sought to change their provincial status from being merely the shogun's appointed governor (*shugo*) or his deputy governor (*shugodai*) to becoming the territory's actual ruler (*sengoku daimyo*, 'lord of the warring states'). With the times as they were, it may have seemed a natural progression to make the transition from governor to ruler, but, in some provinces, things went much further so that certain of the shogun's deputies would return home after living the high life in Kyoto to find that they had been ousted in their absence. Others suffered the greater pain of being ousted in their presence

---

1 Stephen Turnbull, *The Ōnin War 1467-77: A Turning Point in Samurai History* (Warwick: Helion and Company, 2021).

by former followers who had once pledged eternal loyalty to them, or even to be murdered by hitherto unknown local gangsters (the term is by no means entirely inappropriate) who had seized their master's castle, built up a private army and were already behaving like lords of the manor.

History has provided a name for this time of upheaval and for the process that was taking place. The period that followed the Ōnin War would become known as the Sengoku Jidai ('The Age of Warring States'), a term borrowed from ancient China, and the process would be named *gekokujō*: 'the low overcome the high'. Thus, it was in Owari province that the high – the aristocratic Shiba family, on whom the favour of the shogun had rested for many years as *shugo* – would be supplanted by the lower orders in the form of the Oda. Yet this is not to say that the Oda were mud-grubbing peasants, far from it. As loyal and doughty samurai, they had been trusted sufficiently by the Shiba to have been placed in a position of considerable influence in Owari while their masters played the classic role of absentee landlords in the heady atmosphere of elegant Kyoto. Nor was there any single dramatic coup by which the Shiba were overcome. Instead, the Oda simply took advantage of several succession disputes within the house of Shiba to reinforce their own position in the province and to diminish that of their nominal overlords. Indeed, the Shiba would survive in Owari until the 1560s when their last representative was forced to flee, but, by that time, Owari had already been Oda territory for decades.

One of the classic images of traditional samurai warfare is the depiction of a dense hail of arrows, as shown here in an illustration from *Taiheiki Yuei*. Among the achievements popularly credited to Nobunaga was the successful introduction of firearms in place of bows.

# THE RUTHLESS FOOL

The splitting of the Oda clan into two branches had been one result of the power vacuum created by the Shiba's decline, so, by the 1530s, Owari was divided in quite neat geographical terms between the two entities of the Yamato-no-Kami Oda and the Ise-no-Kami Oda. (The juxtaposition of the name of an unrelated Japanese province with the suffix 'no Kami', which indicated its protector, is merely an honorary title to be found throughout Japanese history.) Each branch controlled about half of Owari, with the Yamato Oda ruling from Kiyosu castle and the Ise Oda from Iwakura. Nobunaga's father, Nobuhide, belonged to a subdivision of the Yamato Oda, whose main lineage they challenged from their own headquarters at Shobata. That had partly been achieved by political and economic means, but the main way to gain power in Sengoku Japan was always to wage war, an art at which Oda Nobuhide had long excelled. The main focus for his aggression would eventually be other people called Oda, but Nobuhide's military influence was honed most effectively when he challenged notable opponents who lived outside Owari.

Two daimyo in particular fell into this category. The first lay to the north in the person of Saitō Dōsan Toshimasa (1494–1556) of Mino province, whose position had been the consequence of a classic act of *gekokujō*. Dōsan had been ordained as a Buddhist monk (hence his Dharma name 'Dōsan'), and, according to popular tradition, on leaving the monastery, he married the daughter of an oil seller. The itinerant lifestyle necessitated by that role eventually led him to Mino and military service under its ruler, Toki Yorinari (1502–1582). The *gekokujō* happened when Dōsan overthrew Yorinari and secured his lord's banishment from Mino, after which he seized his territory. Nobunaga's biographer Ōta Gyūichi clearly disapproves of Dōsan, claiming that he executed petty criminals by having them pulled apart by oxen while their families were boiled to death in huge

Saitō Dōsan, the 'Viper of Mino', became Nobunaga's father-in-law and forged a strong alliance with him that greatly helped Nobunaga take over Owari province. (ETKK 1855)

# ODA NOBUNAGA: SAMURAI COMMANDER 1534–82

Imagawa Yoshimoto of Mikawa province, who posed the deadliest threat of all to the Oda clan's southeastern border. (ETKK 1855)

cauldrons.[2] Other anecdotes about Dōsan's ruthlessness gave him the nickname of the Viper of Mino.

The other outside threat to Oda Nobuhide sprang from a very different pedigree. Imagawa Yoshimoto (1519–1560) was not a tradesman but a respected provincial lord descended from an ancient family who had served successive shoguns as *shugo* in the older, pre-Sengoku style. He therefore enjoyed a very different social status from Dōsan and lauded it over the three provinces of Mikawa, Tōtōmi and Suruga along the Pacific coast to the east of Owari. Yoshimoto's most recent forebears had been noted aesthetes and patrons of the arts, to the extent that scenic spots in their ancestral province of Suruga were named after famous places in Kyoto. Yet even the Imagawa had suffered from the upheavals that followed the Ōnin War, because Yoshimoto's father had only succeeded to the family headship owing to the military skills exercised on his behalf by a comparatively lowly samurai who would later be known by the name of Hōjō Sōun. Now, with the growing power of the Hōjō securing his eastern flanks, this latest manifestation of Imagawa greatness could afford to be noble, powerful and ambitious.

## Oda Nobuhide and Son

Displaying the confident style that would become the hallmark of his son Nobunaga, Oda Nobuhide went to war with these two formidable neighbours to secure the borders of his domain. Success would attend his ventures when he managed to establish Oda outposts in enemy territory and retain them against counterattacks, as an early example from 1542 illustrates. During a previous expedition, the bold Nobuhide had entered deeply into the Imagawa territory of Mikawa and had taken a fortress called Anjō. In 1542, the Imagawa took the initiative to win it back, and the two

---

2  CLN 2011, p.101.

armies clashed at the battle of Azukizaka. The fighting was fierce, with records of wounds and deaths being inflicted by Nobuhide's finest warriors who became known as 'the Seven Spears of Azukizaka'. Anjō was saved, and the Imagawa forces withdrew from the vicinity, leaving the Oda in charge of a valuable piece of Imagawa territory. This form of border warfare would become the norm both for Nobuhide and his foes.³

Nobuhide's most famous son was still a child when the battle of Azukizaka took place, and it would not be until the year 1546 that he performed the traditional ceremony of manhood and received the name of Oda Nobunaga. Within a year of that event, Nobunaga took part in his first campaign: a raid into Mikawa, accompanied by a handful of senior retainers who would follow him into battle for many years to come. *Shinchō-Kō ki* tells us that he rode a horse that was itself armoured: an unusual practice at this time in samurai history. His followers set fire to various places as earnest of their intentions and withdrew the next day. That was the common pattern for a Sengoku raid, which not only inflicted some material damage on one's rival but also caused psychological damage when they asserted their impunity by riding unmolested through enemy territory. The Anglo-Scottish border raids of the sixteenth century were no different in either form or intention.

It was soon Mino province's turn to receive Oda Nobuhide's attentions, and it is more than likely that Nobunaga accompanied his father on those expeditions as well, although *Shinchō-Kō ki* does not mention any individual exploits by him. One particular raid followed a similar pattern to Nobunaga's baptism of fire in Mikawa but had a very different outcome. Nobuhide had penetrated Mino province as far as the Saitō headquarters of Inokuchi on the mountain of Inabayama. The wooden fortress of Inokuchi would have been largely a lookout point and a final refuge in times of war, while the daimyo lived in a defended mansion at the foot of the hill in a typical prototype of the castle town. Nobuhide burned the settlements round about and attacked the Inabayama complex as it was growing dark. He then began to withdraw, at which point Saitō Dōsan counterattacked in force. The Oda line crumbled, and more than 5,000 men were killed, including Nobuhide's younger brother. An ignominious retreat and much soul-searching followed.

Encouraged by his success, in late 1547, Dōsan moved against the Oda possession of Ōgaki, which he had previously lost in an Oda raid similar to that which had given them Anjō in Mikawa. Nobuhide cleverly countered the move by making a wide sweep into Mino using a ferry across the river and attacking Dōsan from the rear. The burning of buildings caused sufficient disturbance and commotion for Dōsan to withdraw his forces from Ōgaki. Nobuhide must have been greatly heartened by the resilient Oda presence established in both these enemy territories, but his strategy of cross-border raiding of course obliged him to leave his own half of Owari province less well defended at these times, a situation that would

---

3   CLN 2011, pp.53–54.

be exploited by rivals from his own clan. On one occasion, the leader of the Ise Oda attacked his castle of Furuwatari and burned the environs while Nobuhide was fighting in Mino. That was the start of open hostilities between the two Oda branches, although happily this initial flare-up would be concluded by a peace settlement.

Raids like these were one means of conducting relations with a neighbour during the Sengoku Period, but, when warfare did not succeed, wise alliances could yield equally important political gains, and a very common means of securing a rewarding and peaceful settlement was through a marriage contract, particularly when a clan's long-term future was being considered. The raid on Furuwatari by the Ise Oda had concentrated Nobuhide's mind about what might happen when he died, and very similar thoughts would have been going through the mind of Saitō Dōsan. The latter had of course obtained his position as daimyo by *gekokujō*, an act that could of course be repeated against him, although Dōsan was more fearful about being overthrown not by his followers but by Saitō Yoshitatsu (1527–1561), the son he had adopted when he had failed to produce an heir. As had happened on other occasions in Japanese history, more children were eventually produced, as a result of which Dōsan planned to disinherit Yoshitatsu.

An armour of *dō-maru* style, typical of the times of Oda Nobunaga. (ColBase: Integrated Collections Database of the National Institute for Cultural Heritage, Japan)

Thus, it came about that similar fears about the future of both the Oda and the Saitō families led Nobuhide's skilled negotiator Hirate Masahide (1492–1553) to secure a marriage alliance between Dōsan's daughter, Nōhime, and Nobuhide's heir, Nobunaga. In 1548, the girl moved to Owari as Nobunaga's bride. She was effectively a hostage against any treacherous moves by her brother against her father Dōsan, whose interests Oda Nobuhide now clearly espoused. It was an important development, but very little is known about the woman at the centre of the deal. Nōhime's eventual fate is lost to history; it is not even known if she produced any children by Nobunaga, and she was in any case sent back to Mino when Dōsan died, so her role may best be seen as that of a pawn in Sengoku power politics.

## Oda Nobunaga and Military Technology

The *Shinchō-Kō ki* narrative breaks off at this point to provide some fascinating anecdotes about the teenaged Oda Nobunaga, who was physically very active and both an excellent horseman and swimmer. There are also hints of future military accomplishments when his biographer notes that Nobunaga was being tutored in archery and strategy. On one occasion, he watched a training session and concluded that short spears (*yari*) were less effective than long ones. He therefore introduced spears with three to three-and-a-half *ken* shafts (5.4–6.3 metres). That would have made the Japanese *yari* (which were being increasingly wielded by mounted samurai

# THE RUTHLESS FOOL

instead of bows) into a weapon more resembling a European pike, so the best interpretation of this passage is that Nobunaga was taking important steps towards the transformation of infantry warfare by his *ashigaru* (foot soldiers). For decades afterwards, samurai horsemen continued to wield *yari* of a more reasonable length for mounted fighting, but the trend on foot would be towards very long spears, and Nobunaga seems to have been an early convert to the practice.

It is also within the same section of *Shinchō-Kō ki* that Nobunaga's name is first associated with firearms, the weapons to which his military genius is most often linked. By the time of Nobunaga's marriage to Nōhime, only five years had gone by since the semi-legendary arrival on the island of Tanegashima of shipwrecked Portuguese merchants with the first European-style harquebuses (matchlock muskets, or *teppō* in Japanese) to be seen in Japan, although the specimens they brought with them may well have been manufactured in Southeast Asia. It is now largely accepted that other means of transmission of the innovative weapons had occurred sometime during the 1540s – probably through Japanese pirates with their links to China and Southeast Asia – but, whatever may have been the guns' ultimate origins, *Shinchō-Kō ki* indicates that this latest form of firearms technology had reached Owari by 1548.[4] In that year, young Nobunaga was being trained in harquebus use by a gunnery master called Hashimoto Ippa.[5] *Kunitomo teppō ki* (an imaginative history of the gunsmiths of Kunitomo that was compiled in 1633) goes much further, because its fanciful narrative claims that Nobunaga ordered Hashimoto Ippa to commission 500 harquebuses from Kunitomo for the Oda armoury in 1549.[6] It is difficult to envisage

A striking image of a samurai armed with a *kanasaibō* (studded wooden and iron club) and carrying a severed head. (ETK 1799, detail edited)

---

4  Udagawa Takehisa, *Teppō denrai: heiki ga kataru kinsei no tanjō* (Tōkyō: Kōdansha, 2013), p.13.
5  SKK 1965, p.26.
6  Olof G. Lidin, *Tanegashima: The Arrival of Europe in Japan* (Copenhagen: Nias

# ODA NOBUNAGA: SAMURAI COMMANDER 1534–82

The famous incident whereby shipwrecked Portuguese traders brought the first *teppō* (harquebuses) to Japan in 1543. (ETK 1799, detail)

the 15-year-old Nobunaga having the appropriate authority to do this, although it is perfectly possible that his father could have placed such an order because Kunitomo lay in the adjacent province of Ōmi. If so, it would have placed the Oda right at the forefront of the introduction of firearms to warfare, because 1549 is commonly accepted as the year when harquebuses were first used in anger in Japan.[7]

In spite of this positive claim, the earliest date linking the Oda to firearms in warfare shows the family having guns used against them. According to *Mikawa Monogatari* (which was written in 1622), on 16 June 1549, Imagawa Yoshimoto's uncle and chief strategist, the Zen monk Taigen Sessai (1496–1555), led an army against Nobunaga's brother Nobuhiro in Anjō castle and 'attacked from four directions with arrows and *teppō*'.[8] We may assume that Nobuhiro fired back, but, at the very least, we can say that firearms were well established in the general area of Owari and Mikawa by about 1549 or 1550 and that the Oda family, including the adolescent Nobunaga, were well aware of their potential.

Of equal interest to the accounts of Nobunaga's precocious military skills are the references in *Shinchō-Kō ki* to his character and oddball behaviour. The word Ōta Gyūichi uses to describe him translates as 'fool', but we must remember the distinction the English language makes between being a fool and acting the fool, so the modern reader may see more of the typical teenager in his actions! Gyūichi tends to reinforce a more lordly view when he contrasts Nobunaga's demeanour with that of people 'who still paid attention to correct behaviour', and it is also very noticeable how 'un-Japanese' are the things that Nobunaga gets up to when out in the street. His dress is challengingly casual and is combined with a large intimidating sword thrust through his belt. His hair is tied straight up like a tea-whisk, which is not the style one would expect from a son of a daimyo. He eats in public with no trace of embarrassment, and his alfresco appetite includes rice cakes and even melons. Most un-Japanese of all, Nobunaga invades people's private space by leaning on others as he walks along or hanging

---

Press, 2002), pp.134–35.
7 Stephen Turnbull, 'Biting the Bullet: A Reassessment of the Development, Use and Impact of Early Firearms in Japan', *Vulcan*, 8 (2020), pp.33–34.
8 Suzuki Masaya, *Teppō to Nihonjin* (Tokyo: Chikuma Shobō, 2000), pp.41–42.

# THE RUTHLESS FOOL

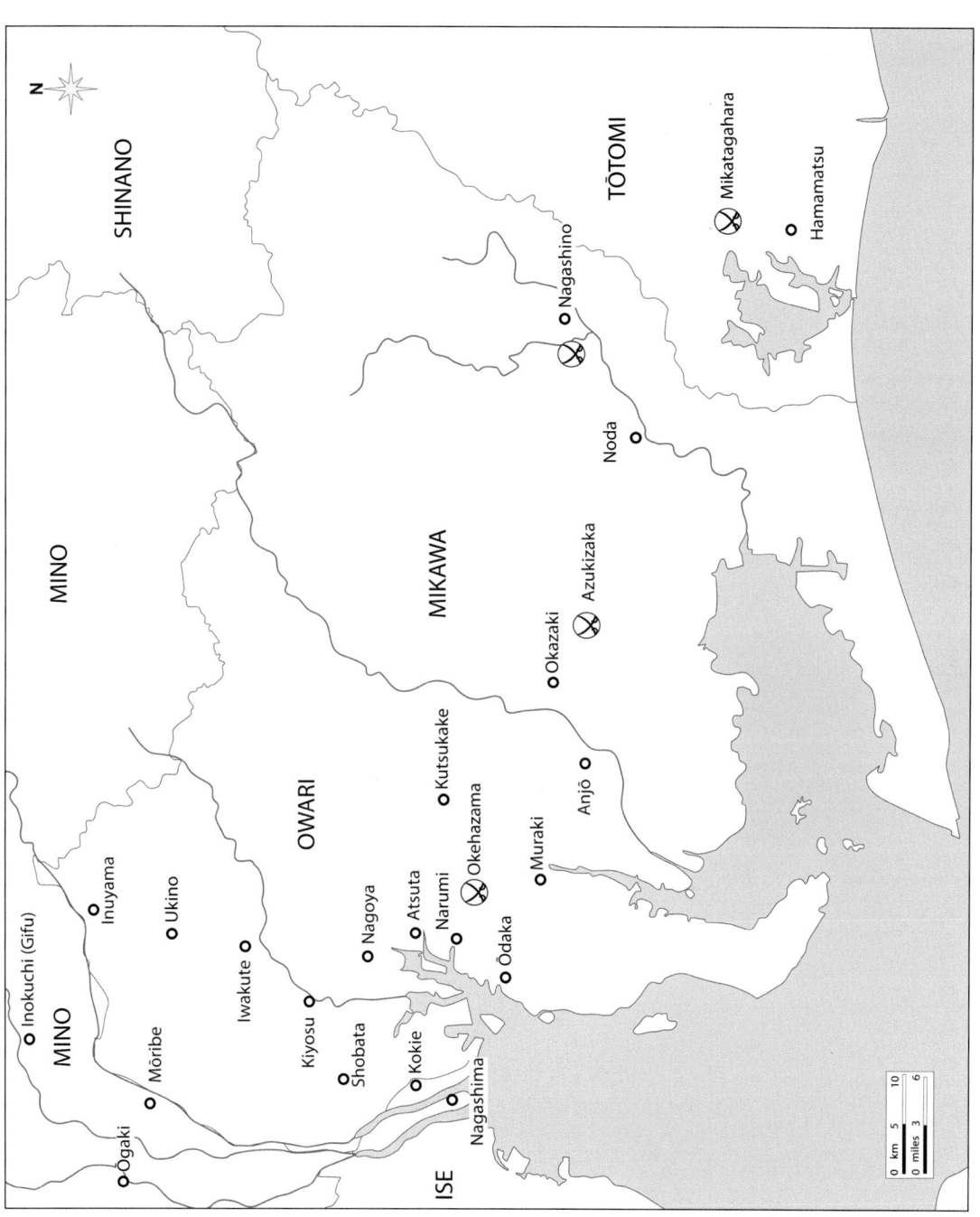

Owari, Mino and Mikawa provinces, showing Oda Nobunaga's realm, c. 1560–1575.

on to their shoulders. All in all, he presents to the world the spectacle of an attention-seeking lout.⁹

## Nobunaga the Disputed Heir

While Nobunaga was playing the fool, his father was preoccupied with the serious business of defending their domain, and, sometime around 1538, he relocated his headquarters farther inland to Nagoya. By 1542, he had given Nagoya to the child Nobunaga and moved again to Furuwatari. Towards the end of the 1540s, Nobuhide moved for a third and final time to Suemori, and *Shinchō-Kō ki* locates him there when he repulses a raid launched on 14 February 1549 by enemies from the other branch of the Oda. Nobuhide was also in Suemori castle when he breathed his last in either 1551 or 1552, and Ōta Gyūichi uses the occasion of Nobuhide's funeral to illustrate Nobunaga's inappropriate behaviour at its most challenging. In contrast to his younger brother Nobuyuki (1536–1557/1558),¹⁰ who presents himself in stiff formal dress with the behaviour to match, the named Oda heir, Nobunaga, is still accoutred for the street, and his sole contribution towards the ritual that would ensure the repose of his father's spirit is to grab a handful of incense and throw it on to the altar, after which he leaves the funeral abruptly, to everyone's disgust.

All this was the behaviour not of a worthy successor to his father but that of a careless and self-centred boor, although one visitor to the funeral ceremony is supposed to have remarked that by his actions – which showed not the slightest concern for propriety or the sensitivity of others – Nobunaga was revealing something of his future greatness and the ruthless means by which he would achieve it. Reading between the lines of the incident, one also gets the impression that Nobunaga's succession was opposed even within his own family. Some of the followers he inherited from Nobuhide would later desert him, and Nobunaga's position remained in dispute for several more years to come. As for his loutishness, in 1553, his former tutor and marriage broker, Hirate Masahide, finally despaired of the young heir's outrageous behaviour and protested in the most acute way possible by committing *seppuku* (ritual suicide). Legend has it that Masahide's suicide shocked Nobunaga into a realisation of his responsibilities and an appreciation of how he should discharge them, and it is indeed true that *Shinchō-Kō ki* provides no more examples of Nobunaga the teenage lout spitting out melon seeds in public. Instead, his behaviour after Nobuhide's passing is more conventional although no less assertive, cunning or self-aggrandising, because his bold and challenging demonstrations are now

---

9 CLN 2011, pp.58–59.
10 He was also known as Nobukatsu, but Nobuyuki is preferred to distinguish him from Nobunaga's son of that name.

# THE RUTHLESS FOOL

designed to intimidate an opponent or impress an ally rather than showing townspeople that he was somehow different.

One of the earliest incidents in this vein occurred in June 1553 when Nobunaga's father-in-law decided to investigate his behaviour. Saitō Dōsan was of course fully aware of Nobunaga's unconventional reputation, but he wanted to experience it for himself, so he invited his son-in-law to meet him at the temple of Shōkokuji in Owari. Dōsan was not above using a little intimidation of his own and deployed several hundred well-groomed retainers on the outer veranda of the temple, in front of which Nobunaga would have to pass. Meanwhile, Dōsan concealed himself within a hut along the way so that he might have a sneak preview of his outlandish son-in-law. Nobunaga arrived dressed in the sartorial combination of sword, tea whisk pigtail and vulgar clothes that Dōsan had been expecting and that confirmed all his worst fears, but, when Nobunaga reached the gate of the Shōkokuji, he had screens erected around him and did a quick-change routine, emerging with a conventional samurai-style folded pigtail, formal court trousers and a short sword. Properly dressed, he then ascended the steps of the temple to meet Dōsan as his father-in-law's equal both in rank and appearance.

This print depicts the moment when Saitō Dōsan (who has concealed himself behind a door!) catches a preliminary glimpse of his notorious son-in-law, Oda Nobunaga. Dōsan was very impressed by Nobunaga's army, who are shown here inaccurately in nineteenth-century uniforms. (Wikimedia Commons)

A further gesture of defiance was made by the composition of Nobunaga's entourage, because he rode at the head of an army about 700–800 strong, although Ōta Gyūichi confuses the reader over the number by claiming that they carried five hundred 6.3-metre-long spears with vermilion shafts and 500 bows and harquebuses. This passage in *Shinchō-Kō ki* is regularly cited to indicate Nobunaga's early grasp of firearms technology, even though the original text does not specify what proportion of the latter 500 weapons were guns. The forceful impression he gave therefore derived mainly from Nobunaga's command of a sizeable and well-turned-out army, and, as for innovative weapons, Dōsan

19

certainly noted the greater length of Nobunaga's spears, which seem to have impressed him more than the harquebuses.[11] It was therefore a very positive experience in every way for Nobunaga, and Dōsan also reprimanded a certain retainer of his who referred to Nobunaga as a fool. Those days had passed.

## Nobunaga's Earliest Military Organisation

The figures quoted above for Nobunaga's entourage in 1553 require further exploration, because, by this date, he was well on the way to becoming an established leader in the footsteps of his father. Sengoku armies like theirs were created through a complex mechanism of obligations, which took into account the relationship of an individual to the head of the family by birth, marriage or adoption, or by different tiers of either hereditary vassalage or submission following defeat or surrender. In this, the system paralleled the lord–vassal relationship in European feudalism.

Closest of all to any daimyo were his *ichimon* (blood relatives). Adoption allowed the entry of allies into the family or the control of other families by placing one's own kinsmen therein, but, in many cases, the swearing of oaths of vassalage was often considered a more trustworthy bond than either kinship or adoption. These non-familial categories could be either *fudai* (loyal hereditary retainers), *tozama* ('outer lords' taken on more recently and whose loyalty could still be questionable) or *kokujin* (smaller landowners from within the lord's territory). An élite group that could be drawn from any of these three categories were the *karō* (elders or senior vassals), who made up an inner council for administration and military policy. They also formed part of the *hatamoto* (literally 'under the standard'), the household troops directly accountable to the daimyo and of whom the élite *umamawari-shū* (Horse Guards) were the most important.

The first *karō* to serve under Oda Nobunaga were four retainers assigned to him by his father in 1540. They were beside Nobunaga at crucial moments in his life, from attending him on his first battle to accompanying him at Nobuhide's funeral. The figure of 800 men was quoted above for 1553 for Nobunaga's army at the time, but two actions during 1554 reveal that, even within one year, Nobunaga's core of 800 men was not sufficient for all the tasks he was now taking on, although he was well supported in various ways. For example, when the Imagawa made common cause with the rival Oda faction, Nobunaga asked for and received 1,000 men from Saitō Dōsan as reinforcements. The marriage alliance was clearly working, and, later in the same year, a retainer of his brother Nobuyuki called Shibata Katsuie (1522–1583) supplied troops to help Nobunaga with an attack on Kiyosu. That is the first mention we have of someone who would play a major role in Nobunaga's future career.

---

11   CLN 2011, pp.61–63.

# THE RUTHLESS FOOL

## Nobunaga Takes Over Owari

With the Saitō alliance secure for now, Nobunaga could concentrate on establishing his rightful position as Nobuhide's heir and extending his hegemony over the entire province of Owari and the whole of the Oda family. That would be achieved largely by war, although assassination would also play a part. The warlike side of the activities consisted of more raids and counterraids against Oda rivals and the repelling of incursions from neighbours. The *Shinchō-Kō ki* accounts of these operations are highly detailed but somewhat confusing, because Ōta Gyūichi has a tendency to omit the dates when the encounters occurred. The identity of the protagonists also sometimes has to be inferred from just the names of their castles, so his account of Nobunaga's earliest operations is like a collection of pearls that have fallen off their string. Taken as a whole, however, the following selection from Ōta Gyūichi's catalogue of provincial fighting gives an excellent taste of Sengoku Period strategy and tactics and allows us to begin a true assessment of the young Oda Nobunaga as a future samurai commander.

We begin on 10 May 1552 with a battle between Nobunaga and Yamaguchi Kurōjirō, the commander of the Imagawa outpost of Narumi, which lay furthest inside the part of Owari that was under enemy control. During Nobuhide's lifetime, Kurōjirō had been regarded as loyal to the Oda and had thus provided an example of how complex the web of Sengoku alliances could be, but matters changed when Nobuhide died, because Kurōjirō rebelled against Nobunaga. A fierce battle ensued, and the rivals set up field positions on two hills that were close enough to allow direct observation. Nobunaga commanded a force of 800 men, which was roughly the same number that he had paraded before Dōsan. The armies descended in force and clashed at a place called Akazuka, which cannot be positively identified, and Ōta Gyūichi continues with an interesting insight into the Japanese tradition of taking heads. The battle began with the exchange of a hail of arrows. One of Nobunaga's officers called Arakawa Yojūrō was struck just below the peak of his helmet and fell dead from his horse. That prompted a diversion from the overall conduct of the battle, because, in true samurai style, enemy soldiers jumped upon his corpse to claim the prestigious head as a trophy, some pulling him by the legs and others using his sword hilt as a handhold. Others grabbed on to his head and torso, but Nobunaga's men joined in, and a fierce tussle took place with his own side finally retrieving the body. From that moment on,

Shibata Katsuie, who became one of Nobunaga's most loyal and talented generals, is commemorated here by a statue erected on the site of Kita-no-shō castle in Fukui.

the scene developed into an uncontrolled melee on foot (the horses were allowed to run free), and so intense was the close-quarter fighting that no one now had the leisure to take heads because another enemy would have been upon him while he did so. A pattern developed whereby a samurai would fight in the melee and then retire (if he could), taking up a defensive posture with one knee bent to the ground, ready to re-enter the fray when he got his breath back. Nobunaga lost 30 men in the engagement and had one man captured alive. His side, too, took one prisoner, but, after hours of intense fighting, honour was satisfied on both parties, who, according to Ōta Gyūichi, knew each other well. They therefore disengaged, exchanged their prisoners and welcomed the horses as they trotted back to their masters. Narumi was saved and remained an Imagawa possession, but Yamaguchi's overlord, Imagawa Yoshimoto, was displeased with his performance and summoned him to Suruga, where he required father and son to commit suicide. Narumi was placed under the command of Okabe Motonobu.

On 4 September of that same year, Nobunaga faced his first major challenge from rivals within his own Yamato branch of the Oda, who sent an army from Kiyosu to fight what became known as the battle of Kaizu. The Kiyosu Oda first secured the loyalty of the garrisons of the nearby castles of Matsuba and Fukata by taking hostages from them. Nobunaga responded to the challenge and together with other family members advanced in separate units against the enemy, combining their forces as they drew near. There was then another melee involving individual acts of heroism as the Kiyosu forces were put to flight. One section of Nobunaga's army then marched upon Matsuba and drove the coerced defenders out. They tried to make a stand away from the castle but suffered many casualties at a distance from arrows and bullets. Another unit then moved against Fukata. Nobunaga joined them, and both of the rebel castles surrendered to him. The survivors fled to Kiyosu, at which Nobunaga destroyed all their fields round about. The struggle for Kiyosu castle had begun.

Matters took a huge turn in Nobunaga's favour the following year when Shiba Yoshimune, the surviving lord who still enjoyed the title of *shugo* of Owari, was ousted from Kiyosu by a group of his supposed followers while he was away from the castle on a fishing trip. The coup happened on 20 August 1553 and was totally successful because Kiyosu was being guarded by a token force of old men whom the rebels showered with arrows and took on in individual sword fights. When they realised that further resistance was useless, the aged garrison set fire to the castle and committed *seppuku*. The women of the castle jumped into the moat; some managed to swim to safety, but others drowned. When Shiba Yoshimune heard of what had happened in his absence, he fled to the protection of Nobunaga. The latter of course appreciated the opportunity he had been given to show loyal support for the official representative of the shogun who was now powerless and no threat, so he treated Yoshimune kindly and installed him in a temple with a retinue of his own. Within days, Nobunaga, brimming with righteous indignation, took advantage of the situation. He did not attack Kiyosu in person but sent loyal subordinates on ahead, whose practised use of long spears came into its own on 26 August 1553. The Shiba were honourably avenged by the gesture, and Kiyosu moved closer to being added to Nobunaga's fold.

## The Siege of Muraki

An incident in 1554 provides a further interesting case study of Nobunaga as a leader, and this time he was in arms against the Imagawa once again. His enemies' main objective was Nobunaga's castle of Ogawa, and, to threaten it, they built a new castle at Muraki, at which certain pro-Nobunaga forces at nearby Teramoto castle defected to his foes. Welcome reinforcements from Saitō Dōsan covered Nobunaga's back while he crossed the sea from Atsuta to the Chita peninsula to engage them. He voyaged in a raging storm, a bold gesture that Ōta Gyūichi compares admiringly to similar tactics by the hero Minamoto Yoshitsune during the Gempei War of the twelfth century. Nobunaga landed safely to the southwest of Ogawa castle, where its keeper, Mizuno Nobutomo, was pleased to receive him and briefed Nobunaga about the situation.[12]

This very fine bronze statue of Oda Nobunaga marks the actual site of his castle of Kiyosu.

Nobunaga attacked Muraki castle on 25 February 1554 in a battle that lasted for 10 hours. It is an interesting action, and Ōta Gyūichi begins by giving us useful details of the castle's layout. As Muraki had been built in a hurry, we may envisage it as a *hirajirō* (castle on a plain as distinct from a mountainous *yamashiro*) with a minimum use of stone, and this is how it appears in a modern reconstruction in a book by Fujii Hisao.[13] Ōta Gyūichi states that the north side of the castle was fully protected by a natural barrier and was therefore left undefended. Fujii's reconstruction shows that this natural barrier was in fact the sea. The main gate was on the east with a smaller postern gate on the west, while the south side was heavily fortified and further protected by an extensive moat and ditch. Fujii sensibly envisages two short wet moats coming from the sea with a dry moat in between them round the main gate. Any castle walls are likely to have been open fences on the seaward side and low plastered or wooden planked

---

12   SKK 1965, pp.38–40.
13   Fujii Hisao, *Dokyumento Sengoku Jō* (Tokyo: Kawade Shobo Shinsha, 1965), pp.36–39.

walls topped with shingles for weather protection around the moats. Both would have been raised upon earth embankments rather than stone.

Nobunaga chose to attack Muraki from the landward side even though it was the best defended, and his young samurai tried to outdo each other in crossing the ditch and scaling the ramparts. If they were pushed off, those who survived immediately ran back to try again, so there were many casualties. Yet Nobunaga was not simply callously wasting his men in pointless assaults, because, for the first time in Ōta Gyūichi's narrative, Nobunaga appears to have put firearms into action to cover his soldiers' assaults. He must have been in the thick of the action, because he observed that most of the casualties were being caused by harquebus bullets fired from loopholes in the walls. Three apertures in particular were providing the fiercest fire, and Ōta Gyūichi credits his hero with silencing them personally. Stationing himself on the edge of the moat, Nobunaga kept up a constant individual barrage against the loopholes by exchanging one pre-loaded harquebus for another. Nobunaga's action shows that he appreciated how important it was for harquebuses to maintain a constant fire if they were to overcome the problem of their loading times, but the operation is far from the deployment of rotating volleys. Instead, it is an action typical of the times whereby harquebuses are used either for precision sharpshooting or to produce the hail of bullets so beloved of the contemporary chroniclers.

Nobunaga's personal intervention had the desired effect, and the defenders were forced to keep their heads down while Nobunaga's samurai rushed back across the moat. Ōta Gyūichi names the leaders responsible for the subsequent victory and notes that, because the defenders had put up such an admirable resistance, their lives were spared when Muraki fell. Their pleas for mercy while surrounded by their dead comrades provided a pitiful spectacle, and we note that Nobunaga had tears streaming down his face. The next day, a much less emotional Nobunaga took Teramoto castle, razed it to the ground and exterminated its owners in order to show his vassals the serious consequences of betrayal.[14]

In 1555, Nobunaga finally took possession of Kiyosu castle from the mainstream Yamato Oda and moved there from Nagoya, although the takeover was less of a military operation and more of a coup performed under cover of deceit. Nobunaga's uncle Nobumitsu (1516–1556) acted as a double agent on behalf of his nephew and entered into a false agreement with the castle's senior officials. Nobumitsu thus succeeded in gaining Kiyosu for Nobunaga, after which he accepted Nagoya as a reward for his duplicity, but Nobumitsu did not live long to enjoy his success because he was murdered the following year by one of the former rebels. As cynical as he was ambitious, Nobunaga saw the removal of his once useful uncle as one less potential rival in Owari. During the same operation against Kiyosu, he also forced Oda Nobutomo, the head of the Yamato Kiyosu faction, to commit suicide, thus getting rid of one more hostile Oda.

---

14   SKK 1965, p.40.

Once he was settled in Kiyosu, Nobunaga turned on his other family rivals in force, beginning in 1556 when his younger brother Nobuyuki finally came out in open revolt. The first attempt at rebellion was quashed, but, when Nobunaga received a tip-off from Nobuyuki's retainer Shibata Katsuie in 1557 that Nobuyuki was stirring again, he feigned illness and asked Nobuyuki to visit him. When Nobuyuki arrived at Kiyosu, he was murdered. During 1556 also, Nobunaga was attacked in Kiyosu by his older half-brother Nobuhiro, but that incident ended peacefully with Nobuhiro's surrender and pledge of allegiance after Nobuhiro was besieged in Anjō castle by Nobunaga, whose ruthlessness must have now become evident to all.

The only resistance to Nobunaga's complete takeover of Owari now rested with the Ise Oda branch based in Iwakura, and it is noticeable from these later actions to see how the numbers of Nobunaga's army have grown since eliminating his other family rivals and absorbing their troops. When Nobuyuki was killed, most of the surviving 1,700 joined Nobunaga and swelled his ranks to between 2,000 and 3,000 strong, with whom he attacked the Iwakura Oda in Ukino castle in 1558. The popular notion that defeated samurai would only commit suicide is therefore utterly disproved. We may also note a rise in the quality and professionalism of Nobunaga's followers in the form of a developing officer corps and the beginning of the élite *hatamoto* as either his celebrated Horse Guards or his leading generals. Names who appear at about this time would become very famous in the years to some, such as Shibata Katsuie, Sakuma Nobumori (?–1581), Ikeda Tsuneoki (1536–1584) and others. They became the most loyal of the loyal, and much of Nobunaga's future operational life would be war by delegation, as he showed himself to be a samurai commander who worked through trust. On certain notable occasions, the trust would fail, but otherwise the calculated risk paid off handsomely.

If Ōta Gyūichi is to be believed, the Ise Oda moved first in 1558 and burned down a village near Kiyosu. Nobunaga retaliated by arson attacks of his own around Iwakura and then sensibly pulled his men back from the raid. He had heard rumours that the Iwakura men were planning to seize a Zen temple called the Shōgenji about three kilometres from Kiyosu and turn it into a fortress. Nobunaga sent his troops to mobilise the local villagers, who were ordered to clear a bamboo grove at the Shōgenji that could be used to provide part of its defences. When the Iwakura Oda moved against them, the locals realised that Nobunaga had only sent a force of 83 mounted men and followers against an invasion by 3,000, but Nobunaga himself drilled the farmers into some semblance of a rearguard armed with bamboo spears. This must have acted as a deterrent, because both sides withdrew their armies.

Nobunaga then took the field directly against Iwakura, which was about nine kilometres from Kiyosu, and set up a position at a place called Ukino. The Iwakura Oda advanced out of the castle to engage him on 25 August 1558, at which point an unusual individual combat took place involving a harquebus. The reader will recall that Nobunaga had been tutored in

## ODA NOBUNAGA: SAMURAI COMMANDER 1534–82

The rear view of a remarkable helmet where the bowl is designed to resemble a samurai hairstyle complete with pigtail and headband. (ColBase: Integrated Collections Database of the National Institute for Cultural Heritage, Japan)

gunner techniques by a certain Hashimoto Ippa. Ippa was a noted warrior, and, when he saw a samurai on the other side called Hayashi Yashichirō, who was fleeing from the field, Ippa pursued him to take his head. They were apparently life-long friends, but all that was forgotten in the heat of battle. Yashichirō loosed an arrow at Ippa and sent it deep into Ippa's armpit, but Ippa was holding a harquebus already loaded with a double charge and primed ready to fire. The bullets knocked Yashichirō to the ground, and one of Nobunaga's *koshō* (pages), a youth called Sawaki Tōhachi, ran forward to take his head. Yashichirō was flat out but managed to unsheathe his sword. He slashed at Tōhachi and cut off his left arm at the elbow. In spite of this, young Tōhachi did not give up but took Yashichirō's head. Not long afterwards, the battle of Ukino ended, and Nobunaga withdrew to Kiyosu.

Early the following year of 1559, Nobunaga began a siege of Iwakura and used firearms in a more conventional way, harrying the defenders with dense volleys of *hiya* (fire arrows) and harquebus bullets, following up the bombardment with infantry attacks. The inner defences now stood alone, because Nobunaga had burned all its outlying settlements and had set up a triple bamboo palisade to confine the defenders into a tight enclosure, so, after several months of pressure, they agreed to surrender. The remnants of the Ise Oda scattered, and Oda Nobunaga was finally master of the entire clan. That was a position he would hold until his untimely death, although his new position did not quite guarantee control of the whole province of Owari. Certain fortresses on his borders were still held by external enemies, as the next chapter will demonstrate.

# 2

# The Road to Okehazama

Throughout the time when he was securing Owari from his own clan members, Nobunaga had to cope with interference from the two great rivals who lay beyond his borders. Saitō Dōsan would of course be placated by marriage, but no comparable option was offered by Imagawa Yoshimoto. As noted above, Yoshimoto held little patches of Owari in the form of frontier forts. Raids and counterraids occurred for several years within the disputed border area, and one such operation would lead to Nobunaga's first famous victory: the decisive battle of Okehazama.

History has not served Imagawa Yoshimoto well, because his undoubted aesthetic sensibilities are routinely presented not as gifts but as failures of character in a military man. Such observations become particularly acute when they are used to contrast him with the supposed military genius of the down-to-earth and practical Oda Nobunaga. In that scenario, any images of Nobunaga as a loutish fool are conveniently forgotten when he is compared to the popular caricature of Yoshimoto as a weak and effeminate daimyo who was better suited to the role of a courtier than that of a samurai. It was noted, for example, that Yoshimoto preferred to be taken to a battlefield in an ornate palanquin rather than ride on a horse. That was probably no more than a demonstration of the exceptionally privileged rank he enjoyed by virtue of being related to the shogun, but, like so many other things, a soft image is used against him.

Even Yoshimoto's detractors, however, acknowledge that he had an eye for military talent among those who served him, but none was to achieve more fame and greatness than the future shogun Tokugawa Ieyasu (1542–1616). He had begun his service to the Imagawa as a child hostage and fought his first battle for Yoshimoto in 1558. It took the form of a border raid and was directed against the frontier fort of Terabe, which had defected to Oda Nobunaga's side. Terabe lay within Ieyasu's own ancestral territory of western Mikawa, so it was only natural that Yoshimoto should give the job of retaking it to his young protégé. Ieyasu thereupon went to his family's capital of Okazaki and raised an army from loyal family retainers who were eager to serve their young lord, even if it was in the overall interests of their unpopular master Imagawa Yoshimoto.

*Mikawa Gofudo ki* makes much of Ieyasu's baptism of fire and even credits him with outwitting the mighty Oda Nobunaga. Displaying an enthusiasm and recklessness that paralleled the behaviour of the fool of Owari, Ieyasu led the attack personally and took the outer defences of Terabe. The inner stronghold, however, held firm, and Ieyasu realised that he was vulnerable to attack from one or another of Terabe's minor supporting outposts that lay around. His solution was to set fire to the outer defence works and then withdraw under cover of the smoke. An Oda counterattack did occur as he had anticipated, but Ieyasu was prepared for it and drove Nobunaga's men away, after which he retired in good order.

Ieyasu also went into action against Nobunaga the following year in an operation that became known as the Provisioning of Ōdaka. Ōdaka was one of Yoshimoto's key frontier forts in Owari and had passed into his possession when its commander abandoned Nobunaga, leaving it projecting on a salient into Oda territory. Yoshimoto had placed it under the command of Udono Nagamochi, but its isolated position left it open to siege action from a distance because Nobunaga could easily cut off its supplies. Its maintenance was therefore crucial to Yoshimoto's plans for a serious large-scale advance into Owari the following year.

To escort a baggage train of pack animals under fire was not among the highest personal goals sought by an up-and-coming leader of samurai, but Ieyasu behaved with due deference. Assessing the situation, he divided his forces into three. Two units would launch diversionary attacks against Nobunaga's forts of Terabe and Umezu, while the third would lie concealed until midnight with the baggage train hidden within their ranks rather than bringing up the rear of the army as was usual. Under the cover of darkness, Ieyasu approached to within two kilometres of Ōdaka, at which attacks were launched on Terabe and Umezu with as much noise and commotion as possible. The ruse succeeded beyond even Ieyasu's wildest dreams, because not only did these two fortresses become fully preoccupied by the attack but also two other Oda forts at Washizu and Marune immediately sent troops to their assistance. With all four hostile positions neutralised, Ieyasu calmly led his 1,200 pack horses into Ōdaka unmolested.

## Yoshimoto's Owari Campaign

The provisioning of Ōdaka would be Yoshimoto's final preliminary operation against the frontier forts, because, as the 1550s drew to a close, he began planning a major operation to take Owari and destroy Oda Nobunaga once and for all. Yoshimoto certainly had the military strength to achieve his aims. His rear was secure, sustained by a tripartite alliance involving the Takeda and the Hōjō clans that had been brought about with the help of a marriage between Hōjō Ujiyasu's daughter and Imagawa Yoshimoto's heir, Ujizane. Yoshimoto had clearly demonstrated an ability to capture the frontier forts, so the stage was set for the first major clash between the two hostile neighbours, although Yoshimoto's overall aims are popularly misunderstood. It is often claimed that his journey along the Tōkaidō (the Pacific coast road) from Suruga was in fact the start of a long march against Kyoto, where Yoshimoto intended to become the first daimyo to make the shogun bend to his will. That may well have been Yoshimoto's ultimate life goal (he never lived to confirm it), but the 1560 operation had as its target Kiyosu not Kyoto, and Nobunaga was much more than just an inconvenient obstacle along the way.

Interestingly, Yoshimoto's Owari campaign also involved the participation of all three of Japan's future unifiers, because serving in the Oda army was Nobunaga's ultimate successor, Toyotomi Hideyoshi (1536–1598), who was then just a lowly samurai in Oda service. Hideyoshi acted as Nobunaga's sandal bearer, a post equivalent to a daimyo's batman, and legend tells us that he endeared himself to his master by warming Nobunaga's straw sandals inside his own shirt during wintertime. Hideyoshi's own successor, Tokugawa Ieyasu, who restored the shogunate in 1603, was of course on the opposing side, supporting Imagawa Yoshimoto as he proceeded to win every battle of the campaign except the last.

Full accounts of the Owari campaign and the famous battle of Okehazama by which it ended appear in both *Shinchō-Kō ki* and *Mikawa Gofudo ki*. The latter account is the best-known version, whereby Yoshimoto captures Nobunaga's forts and then foolishly allows himself to be taken by surprise when he rests his army. *Shinchō-Kō ki* follows the same outline but differs slightly in several interesting ways. Whereas *Mikawa Gofudo ki* places the greatest emphasis on Nobunaga's decision to make one overwhelming assault on Yoshimoto's camp, *Shinchō-Kō ki* describes earlier attacks being launched, which suggests that Yoshimoto was not totally unaware of Nobunaga's presence. Both, however, agree on the enormity of Nobunaga's victory, although only *Shinchō-Kō ki* dares to hint at the callous reasoning that may have lain behind the perplexing attitude and behaviour that Nobunaga displayed before the great battle took place, as will be revealed later.

The *Shinchō-Kō ki* account begins by explaining how the network of border forts played a key part in Yoshimoto's plan. None had been established at random by either the Oda or the Imagawa, because each had a strategic role in guarding a crucial road, river or estuary or had been built simply as a counter to an enemy outpost that had already secured such an advantage. The most forward position that Yoshimoto controlled was Narumi, where the high tides of the estuary lapped at the castle's outer defences. Unable to overcome Narumi, Nobunaga had countered its presence by building the three forts of Nakashima, Tange and Zenshōji, the last of which was raised on the ruins of a Buddhist temple. On the opposite side of the estuary lay the Oda outposts of Washizu and Marune, which had been built similarly as counters to Yoshimoto's Ōdaka. To make any headway into Owari and capture Kiyosu, Imagawa Yoshimoto's army had to destroy or seize the hostile forts once and for all.

*Shinchō-Kō ki* reports that, after leaving Suruga, Yoshimoto's main body marched as far as the castle of Kutsukake, his furthest forward strongpoint

# ODA NOBUNAGA: SAMURAI COMMANDER 1534–82

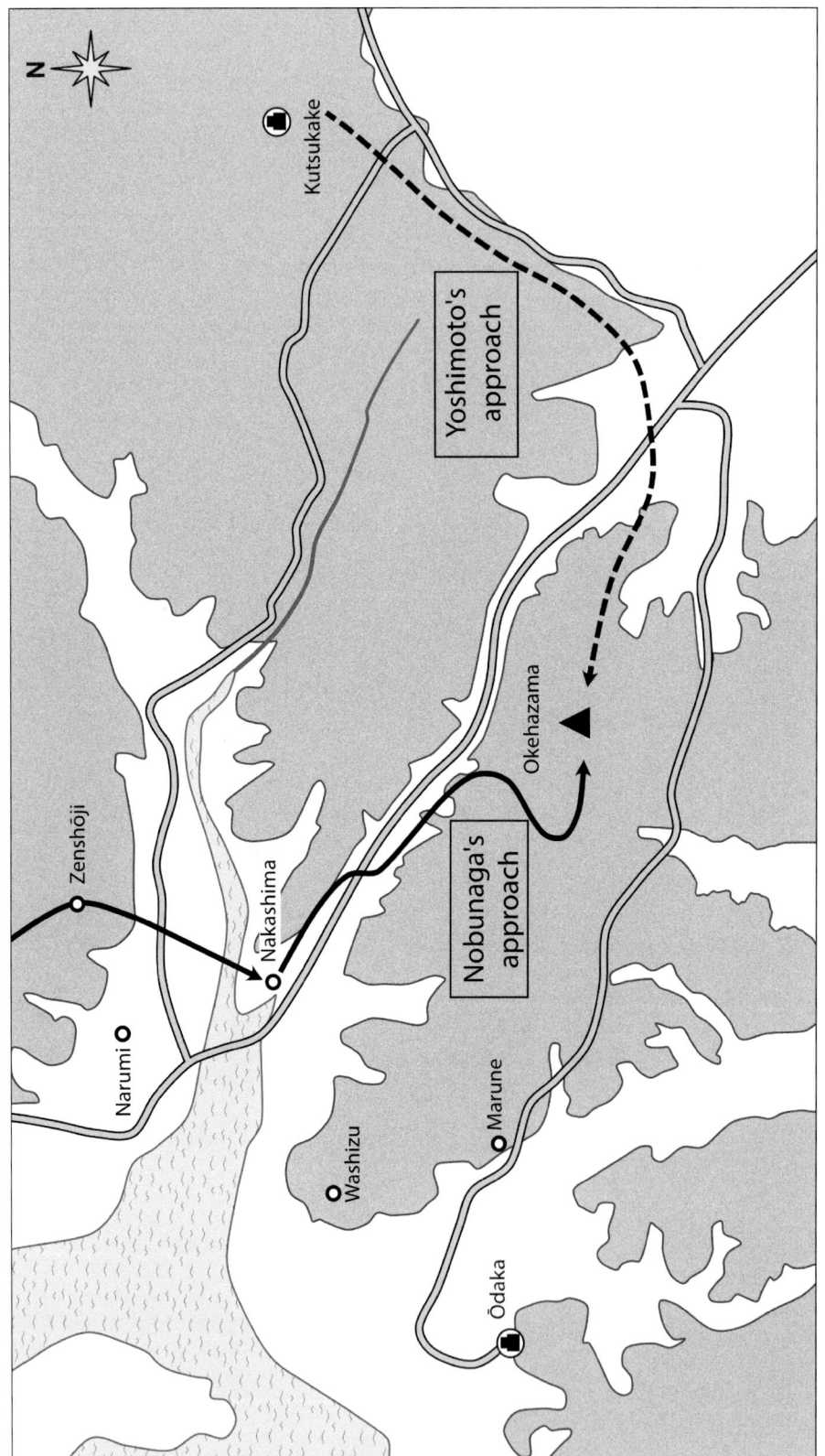

The frontier fortresses and the Okehazama Campaign, 1560.

before the immediate frontier area. He then sent advance units on ahead to strengthen his key position of Ōdaka, and the first shots of the campaign were fired against the Oda fortress of Marune. The task of reducing it had fallen to Tokugawa Ieyasu, and *Mikawa Gofudo ki* provides the fullest account because its hero is in action. First, he made a sharp attack, at which the defenders opened the gate and sallied out to find Ieyasu waiting for them with volleys of arrows and bullets. One of the rounds may even have been responsible of the death of Nobunaga's castle commander Sakuma Daigaku. That was Sadler's interpretation of the original sources, which do not specifically state that Sakuma was shot dead. If he was, then Sakuma would have been the first named high-ranking samurai in history to be felled by a harquebus ball.[1] Ieyasu went on to attack Washizu, which suffered the same fate as Marune, although we know no details of the action. He was commended by Yoshimoto for his victories and ordered to rest his men and horses inside Ōdaka, where he was to assume command and defend the vital fort against any possible counterattack. In view of what happened next, it was an order that may well have saved Ieyasu's life.

Imagawa Yoshimoto was now effectively in control of the eastern arm of the estuary with two hostile fortresses captured and Ōdaka intact. Because of the speed of contemporary communications, Marune and Washizu had both fallen by the time that their keepers' pleas for assistance had reached Nobunaga in Kiyosu. He apparently reacted to the out-of-date news in a manner that alarmed his followers, because he treated Yoshimoto's advance with a surprising nonchalance and a total absence of panic. Nobunaga's generals were also left in ignorance as to what their master's plans actually were because he called no council of war. It would appear that Nobunaga had already worked out his own secret strategy.

Nobunaga also took his time before leaving for battle and in fact impressed his immediate followers by treating them to a solemn performance of a classic chant from the Noh play *Atsumori*, which deals with the tragic death of the young hero Taira Atsumori at the battle of Ichinotani in 1184. The stanzas referred to the brevity of human existence, which is so short as to make one's life look like a dream or an illusion. It was the experience of every human, because everyone born has to die. A solemn recitation like this was not the behaviour of a young fool!

When he finished the dance drama, Nobunaga ate some breakfast, ordered the *horagai* (war conch) to be blown as a signal for an immediate advance, got into his armour and set off to meet the greatest challenge that the Oda had ever faced, but Nobunaga's journey from Kiyosu to the front line was equally lacking in panic. The route took him past the great shrine of Atsuta, the home of the sacred sword from the Japanese imperial regalia and the holiest place in Owari. Nobunaga, always the master of the moment, knew the value of symbolism, so he prayed for the assistance of the *kami*

---

1  A. L. Sadler, *The Maker of Modern Japan: The Life of Tokugawa Ieyasu* (London: Allen and Unwin, 1937), p.53; KMGF 1976, vol. 1, p.216.

(deity) Atsuta Daimyōjin in the battle to come. Nobunaga's method was to deposit a written prayer for victory that denounced Yoshimoto as a villain who invaded other people's territories and despoiled shrines. With Owari's spiritual welfare thus secure, Nobunaga rode off with the same nonchalant air that he had displayed since receiving what was to all intents and purposes very bad news, because two forts had been lost and a hostile army was advancing that outnumbered the Oda force by a reliable estimate of 12 to one.

After passing the fort of Tange, Nobunaga stopped at Zenshōji. There, he grouped his men into a conspicuous combat formation to give the impression that he was either planning to resist Yoshimoto's advance from there, attack Narumi or at the very least cut Narumi off from support. The move also suggested that Nobunaga was not planning to advance any further towards Yoshimoto for the time being. Nobunaga's advance to Zenshōji and his battle deployment had been spotted by the Imagawa scouts, so Yoshimoto was not at all surprised when he received the first attack of the campaign by some outlying Oda samurai who had launched a probing raid. They were driven off very successfully with 50 casualties among the Oda force, so Yoshimoto was even more convinced that Nobunaga would not advance any further. Understandably pleased at how things were going, the elegant Yoshimoto recited his own selection from the Noh repertoire to celebrate. Claiming that neither devils nor demons could stand up to him, he began to relax.

Nobunaga, however, had already moved up to the fortress of Nakashima, which had now become his forward position. Still ignorant of Nobunaga's overall strategy, his immediate subordinates expressed grave concern about making any further advance, but Nobunaga would not listen to them and at last gave public expression to his own understanding of the situation. His belief was that, having gained a number of victories and having carried out the task of reinforcing Ōdaka, Yoshimoto's army would be tired. Nobunaga would hit them while they rested in the illusion that Nobunaga was still waiting for them in battle order somewhere near Narumi.

The decision that now had to be made was where to strike, and reports had reached Nobunaga that Yoshimoto's army had stopped at a place called Okehazama-yama or Mount Okehazama. That became the target for the subsequent confrontation, but strangely, for so famous a battle, the hill of Okehazama cannot be identified, and even the location of the subsequent engagement is disputed. *Mikawa Gofudo ki* reminds us that it was an area that Nobunaga knew well so that he was able to move in a wide circle to the northeast and deploy his troops to the rear of Yoshimoto's position without being seen. The same chronicle also supplies the information that Yoshimoto is traditionally supposed to have set up camp within a gorge called Dengaku-hazama and not on a mountain at all, which would have been a strange choice for so experienced a leader.

Nobunaga gave strict orders that, when the surprise attack began, his men should keep moving and not pause to collect trophies from the dead. A party of his samurai then returned having done the latter, because they had with them several Imagawa heads from the earlier raid. Nobunaga repeated his new admonition to these men, who joined him for the advance to Okehazama. Very soon, Nobunaga's bold decision to press forward while the captured fortresses lay menacingly to his rear was dramatically confirmed as correct by the grateful deity Atsuta Daimyōjin, who sent a ferocious storm against the area. It was the height of summer, but hailstones pelted down towards the enemy positions, and a great fallen tree symbolically pointed the way towards victory. *Mikawa Gofudo ki* maintains that Yoshimoto was totally preoccupied by the ritual of head-viewing while feasting and drinking and had no idea of Nobunaga's presence until he burst upon the Imagawa encampment like a thundercloud of his own making. *Mikawa Gofudo ki* suggests that Yoshimoto thought a brawl had broken out among his own men. So fierce was Nobunaga's assault that the outer lines of Yoshimoto's defences collapsed entirely, and even his personal attendants abandoned their master's ostentatious palanquin.

The ultimate target of the attack was of course Imagawa Yoshimoto himself, who was well protected within his inner circle of *hatamoto*. They formed a circle around their lord and fought back four or five times against Nobunaga's repeated assaults, but this was Nobunaga's moment, and soon only 50 stalwarts remained in defence within the huge hacking melee. All attention now passed to the ultimate samurai accolade of taking the enemy leader's head. The first to make personal contact with him was Nobunaga's follower Hattori Kazutada, but Yoshimoto fought back well (thus disproving the effete image he would later acquire) and slashed Kazutada across his

As lightning flashes and rain falls, Imagawa Yoshimoto is killed by Nobunaga's troops at the battle of Okehazama in 1560. (ETK 1799)

# ODA NOBUNAGA: SAMURAI COMMANDER 1534–82

Another view of the decisive moment of the battle of Okehazama. The assailant is not identified in the caption but is probably Hattori Kazutada, whom Imagawa Yoshimoto wounded, thus disproving the effeminate image later attributed to him. (KMGF 1886)

kneecaps, making him crash to the ground. Then Mōri Yoshikatsu took over, felled Yoshimoto and cut off his head, although again not without difficulty because a traditional story relates that Yoshimoto bit off one of Yoshikatsu's fingers. Nevertheless, within minutes of it beginning, the battle of Okehazama was over.

No victory in Nobunaga's entire career would ever be as dramatic as Okehazama. It is usually presented as his reward for Yoshimoto's carelessness and lack of military acumen, but it is unlikely that Nobunaga saw it that way or had even planned his strategy on that basis. Imagawa Yoshimoto was a formidable opponent in command of a formidable army, and my personal understanding of Nobunaga's strategy hinges on the fact that he called no war council when his forts were attacked. First, he had no desire to have the details leaked in any way to the enemy; *shinobi* (spies) were everywhere in Sengoku Japan. That was no more than sensible, but it is also likely that he did not want the details to be revealed even to his friends, because I believe that Nobunaga intended all along to sacrifice Washizu and Marune to Yoshimoto as if they were stones in a game of *go*. If he had wanted to save them, he would surely have moved much earlier. Instead, the capture of the forts lulled Yoshimoto into a false sense of security. He had completed his tasks for the day and was therefore vulnerable to a counterattack by fresh troops who knew the terrain and were fortuitously aided by a thunderstorm.

Did Nobunaga have in mind the defeat his father had suffered at Inabayama during the 1540s when the Saitō had counterattacked while the Oda retreated? The parallels are interesting; Nobuhide had been caught off guard and lost 5,000 men.

It is also important to note that Nobunaga was taking quite a risk when he sought confrontation with Yoshimoto, because, with Saitō Dōsan's death in 1556, the marriage contract with Nobunaga had come to an end. Nōhime had been returned to her home province, and Nobunaga found himself at odds with Dōsan's successor, as will be explained later. Also, one little scrap of Owari remained hostile. This was Inuyama on the Kiso River, which would not fall to Nobunaga until 1565. He was therefore forced to advance against Yoshimoto while his rear was less secure than it had been for a decade, so it was fortunate for Nobunaga that Yoshimoto's demise was secured so rapidly.

As it turned out, all the other Imagawa centres of resistance collapsed with the death of their leader. Ōdaka castle, which had been the focal point of Yoshimoto's advance, was abandoned along with Kutsukake, where they had assembled before Okehazama, so all but one of the Imagawa frontier forts had now surrendered. The exception was Narumi, whose commander is said to have been present at the battle of Okehazama and is credited with escaping with Yoshimoto's head instead of letting it fall as a prize to the Oda. His life was spared when he agreed to surrender the castle and hand the head over to Nobunaga. The trophy was carried in triumph in front of Nobunaga's army when they rode back into Kiyosu. It then took pride of place among 3,000 other trophies in a spectacular ritual of head inspection.

Nobunaga's victory would also be shared in an indirect fashion by Tokugawa Ieyasu, who remained inside Ōdaka until the last moment when it was confirmed that his overlord was in fact dead. Ieyasu then withdrew to Okazaki even though he dared not enter his own castle because it was garrisoned by Imagawa men. He even contemplated suicide as the Oda troops drew near. The chief priest of his ancestral temple dissuaded him from that course of action and helped in the resistance, but, when they heard the news of Yoshimoto's death, all the Imagawa samurai began to pull out of Mikawa, and Ieyasu had his freedom for the first time since childhood. The following year, he abandoned Yoshimoto's heir, Ujizane, and allied himself with Oda Nobunaga. The latter's victory at Okehazama was now complete.

# 3

# Nobunaga and the Shogun

Hardly anything has been said up to this point about the shogun, the man who was supposedly the military ruler of Japan. To some extent, this omission reflects the actual historical situation, because, since the Ōnin War, the shogun had carried little weight when it came to directing the paths of the up-and-coming independent provincial daimyo. Yet the old power structure still existed and had somehow retained its magic, so newly powerful warlords like Nobunaga were only too keen to reinforce their local control by accepting a blessing from the ancient central authority of the shogun. In certain cases, this extended to the venerable imperial court, so we read of daimyo visiting the capital and being received in audience by the emperor as well as the shogun, both of whom bestowed upon them grand-sounding but largely meaningless titles. The daimyo would then respond by making rich donations to the imperial and shogun's courts, often for building projects.

    The system brought satisfaction to the shogun in particular, because, as the Sengoku Period got under way, he needed all the friends he could get. The desperate situation in which the shoguns found themselves dated back to the Meiō Coup of 1493, when the reigning shogun had been usurped and exchanged for another, a situation that had never been contemplated even during the worst excesses of the Ōnin War. The eleventh Ashikaga shogun, Yoshizumi (1478–1511), had supposedly been the beneficiary of the coup, but, in reality, he was a puppet of those who had put him in position and would eventually be replaced by his cousin Yoshitane, the tenth Ashikaga shogun, whom Yoshizumi had originally replaced. So things went on, and, by the time of the reign of the twelfth Ashikaga shogun, Yoshiharu (1510–1550), the selection of its incumbent lay totally at the whim of rival daimyo. Matters came to a particularly violent head with the accession of the thirteenth Ashikaga shogun, Yoshiteru (1535–1565), who was appointed at the age of 10 and was almost immediately forced to flee from Kyoto when his father, Yoshiharu, made a deal with the usurpers. When Yoshiharu died, Yoshiteru returned but stayed under the thumb of Miyoshi Chōkei (1523–1564) and Matsunaga Hisahide (1510–1577), Japan's most notorious 'kingmakers'.

To rid himself of their influence, Yoshiteru sought help from outside, and that was where the mutual benefits of the Kyoto-orientation enjoyed by the more astute daimyo came into play. Unfortunately, what the shogun needed was more than mere pledges of support in return for a title. He needed warriors, but those he asked to fight for him tended either to be banished by the shogun's puppet masters or were warned off and refused to get involved in such a dangerous task. It was then that Yoshiteru lighted upon the emerging power of Oda Nobunaga. Hoping to secure his favour, the shogun appointed Nobunaga to the post of *shugo* of Owari province in 1559. The title meant little in military terms to Nobunaga. Its value lay instead in giving him official approval for the complete takeover of his home province, which he would accomplish that year.[1]

The shogun's investiture was the first contact Nobunaga had had with the man who was theoretically his lord and master but very much a tool of his controllers, although it was certainly not the first contact that either the emperor or the shogun had had with the Oda family. In 1540, Oda Nobuhide had made a financial contribution to the rebuilding of the Outer Shrine of Ise and was rewarded by the emperor with the title of Mikawa-no-Kami, an appellation that cannot have gone down well with the Imagawa who actually ruled Mikawa. Two years later, Nobuhide assisted with the cost of repairs to the walls of the imperial palace, and then, in 1559, his son Oda Nobunaga was received in audience by the shogun Yoshiteru, who gave him the title noted above and forged a personal link with someone who could help him in his endeavours. Nobunaga's relationship with the shogun and with the emperor developed from that time onwards and was given a huge boost by his victory at Okehazama, because he was now regarded as a general of the highest calibre whom any shogun would wish to have on his side. Nobunaga also realised that he was moving towards a position whereby he might even march on Kyoto in force and control the shogun. His rear was secure from his alliance with Tokugawa Ieyasu after Okehazama, so only the rulers of two provinces – Mino and Ōmi – could now realistically prevent Nobunaga from entering Kyoto, and, as the 1560s got under way, Mino moved closer towards becoming part of the Oda domain and a vital stepping stone towards Nobunaga's achievement of his goals.

## Nobunaga's Mino War

Mino, of course, had long been the Saitō domain, and, throughout the time of Nobunaga's consolidation of Owari, he had received vital support from his loyal father-in-law, Saitō Dōsan. Dōsan and his army had faithfully covered Nobunaga's back since the time of his marriage, but things began to change in 1556 following a spate of internal bloodletting within the

---

1   Lamers, *Japonius Tyrannus*, p.42.

## ODA NOBUNAGA: SAMURAI COMMANDER 1534–82

Saitō family. Dōsan's adopted son, Yoshitatsu (1527–1561), killed both his brothers and went into open conflict with his father. The loyal Nobunaga supported Dōsan and set off into Mino, but Yoshitatsu defeated Dōsan and killed him at the battle of Nagaragawa on 28 May 1556. Judging by the account in *Shinchō-Kō ki*, there was a fierce competition for his head. One samurai almost succeeded in taking him alive, but another ran up and slashed Dōsan's legs so that he fell and decapitated him. Seeking evidence for his feat, the first of the three to get involved swung his sword at the already severed head and took off Dōsan's nose as proof of his involvement. The patricide Yoshitatsu then challenged Nobunaga, who was forced into a fighting retreat across the Nagaragawa. Nobunaga nobly provided the rearguard for his escaping army and deployed a harquebus on his own, just as he had at Muraki. His sharp shooting skills proved sufficient to persuade the Saitō not to continue their pursuit, but, with Yoshitatsu in charge, Mino had become enemy territory once again.[2]

Matters remained at a stalemate between the Oda and the Saitō until after Okehazama, although history is silent about why they never intervened while Nobunaga was busy with the Imagawa, because he could well have been defeated by a rear attack. The fall of the Iwakura Oda probably had a lot to do with it, but, once the Imagawa threat had been removed, Nobunaga could take on the Saitō at his leisure, and once again we find a further list of

Oda Nobunaga partakes of a cup of water before departing for war. This is an *ema* (votive painting) in a temple in Inuyama. Inuyama castle was one of the last fortresses controlled by the rival Oda faction to fall to Nobunaga.

---

2   SKK 1965, pp.68–69.

border wars and raids. The overall details are somewhat tedious, although the following anecdotes are very revealing about Nobunaga's developing military skills and his application of modern technology and siegecraft. None of Nobunaga's subsequent campaigns, however, was directed against the usurper Saitō Yoshitatsu because he died on 23 June 1561, possibly from the leprosy that he had suffered from for many years. Unfortunately for Nobunaga, Yoshitatsu's successor, Saitō Tatsuoki (1548–1573), proved to be just as redoubtable an enemy for Nobunaga in spite of his youth. In 1561, Nobunaga defeated Tatsuoki at Mōribe in a battle described by Ōta Gyūichi as a gift from heaven where Nobunaga's follower the future daimyo Maeda Toshiie (1538–1599) distinguished himself by taking two heads.

While these operations against Saitō Tatsuoki were continuing, internal opposition was still being pursued by rival Oda members, until Inuyama castle, high on the Kiso River, became the one place in Owari that had still not submitted to Nobunaga. In 1565, Nobunaga took the opportunity to settle the matter and encircled Inuyama with a triple palisade of bamboo. He then attacked two support castles belonging to Inuyama called Uruma and Sarubami. Nobunaga took up a position on a hill visible to both places, and Uruma surrendered merely on seeing Nobunaga's army. Sarubami, too, surrendered when Nobunaga seized an adjacent strongpoint and cut off Sarubami's water supply.

At some stage in this campaign, the Saitō set up a position at the castle of Dōbora. Nobunaga ordered his men to throw burning torches inside the castle's wooden wall, forcing the defenders back into their inner enclosure. The fight is also notable for the personal involvement of Nobunaga's soon-to-be biographer Ōta Gyūichi, who was a highly skilled archer as well as an author and picked off the defenders one by one. The appreciative Nobunaga sent three successive messages of congratulations to him and rewarded Gyūichi with a grant of land, all of which is proudly recorded in *Shinchō-Kō ki*.[3] The Saitō, however, counterattacked and drove Nobunaga away, but the balance of power was to change again when Nobunaga received the defection of three key individuals from Mino: Inaba Ittetsu, Ujiie Naomoto and Andō Morinari, the 'Mino Triumvirs'.

Emboldened by their arrival, Nobunaga moved directly against the Saitō capital on Inabayama. It was a formidable obstacle, and it would appear that Nobunaga captured it once in 1564 only to lose it again, but he retook it in midsummer of 1567 using a clever battlefield trick. When the two armies were arrayed against each other, Nobunaga encircled Tatsuoki's lines under cover of darkness and approached them from behind using false flags of Tatsuoki's followers as a decoy. When Tatsuoki attacked Nobunaga's remaining force, thinking that only his own loyal samurai were standing behind him, Nobunaga attacked from the rear. Tatsuoki escaped by boat. On taking Inabayama, Nobunaga moved his capital there and renamed the place Gifu.

---

3   CLN 2011, p.113.

# ODA NOBUNAGA: SAMURAI COMMANDER 1534–82

By his acquisition of Mino, Nobunaga had become the master of two provinces. That and the victory at Okehazama had given him a reputation that few had ever foreseen for someone they had once dismissed as the fool of Owari, and the conquest of Mino even elicited a message of congratulations from the emperor. It was also a subtle request for Nobunaga to visit Kyoto again, although this time it would not be for a formal audience. To explain why, it will be necessary to backtrack a few years and examine the fate of the shogun who had once received him in solemn state.

## A Lord for a Shogun

While Nobunaga was busy confronting the Saitō, shogun Ashikaga Yoshiteru's end had come at the hands of the men who had put him in post, because, in 1565, Miyoshi and Matsunaga decided to abandon Yoshiteru and replace him with a relative. The act was done with great brutality by means of a surprise night attack against the shogun's palace. Ashikaga Yoshiteru took on his assailants, but, when he was mortally wounded, he crawled into an adjacent room and committed *seppuku*. After this successful part of the coup, the plotters' plans started to fall apart. A lack of imperial support and dissension among the conspirators meant that their nominee for the position of fourteenth shogun – Yoshiteru's distant cousin

A very dramatic and bloodthirsty depiction of the assassination of shogun Ashikaga Yoshiteru. His murder allowed the avenging Nobunaga to move closer towards the centre of power. (EIG 1881)

the infant Yoshihide – was refused investiture. Frustrated in this respect and desperate for time, they resolved to use a different puppet and chose instead Yoshiteru's younger brother Yoshiaki, who was living peacefully at the time as a monk in Nara. The plotters sought out Yoshiaki and pledged that no harm would come to him, but their assurances were not believed, so Yoshiaki slipped away from Nara before they could capture him.

A hopeless fugitive, Ashikaga Yoshiaki sought refuge with a succession of daimyo whose names will figure prominently in the pages that follow. He first found sanctuary with the minor landowner Wada Koremasa, who was too weak to help Yoshiaki achieve his goals, so Yoshiaki moved on to Ōmi and the protection of Rokkaku Jōtei Yoshikata (1521–1598), whom he believed would escort him to Kyoto to claim his throne. It was a sensible choice, because the Rokkaku had made a successful transition from *shugo* to daimyo and now ruled their territories from Kannonji castle, which was built on a distinctive mountain that soared out of the flat plain near Lake Biwa. He and his son were militarily strong, but they proved unwilling to risk the good relationship they enjoyed with the Miyoshi faction and soon sent Yoshiaki on his way again. As *Shinchō-Kō ki* puts it so well, 'The tree Yoshiaki had sought to shelter under was letting the rain in'.[4] The desperate Yoshiaki then sought help from Asakura Yoshikage (1533–1573) of Echizen province. Yoshikage gave him a temporary refuge but rejected any notion of helping Yoshiaki become shogun.

Ashikaga Yoshiaki, the fifteenth and last of the Ashikaga shoguns, who became a fugitive and would finally be put into position by Nobunaga in 1568. This wooden statue of him is at the Tōji-In in Kyoto.

---

4  SKK 1965, p.83.

## ODA NOBUNAGA: SAMURAI COMMANDER 1534–82

There was now only one nearby daimyo left: Oda Nobunaga of Owari. After much thought, Nobunaga pledged his support because he realised that Yoshiaki could help serve his own ambitions, which he had already expressed in words on his official seal as *tenka fubu*: 'Rule the Empire by Force', but to fully control the shogun was a goal that other daimyo had only dreamed of. Miyoshi and Matsunaga had actually made it happen for a while, but their position was precarious, and, if Nobunaga could get rid of them and their own nominee, the glittering prize could be his. The wretched Yoshiaki probably knew that also, but he was forced into Nobunaga's arms.

For Yoshiaki to become shogun, he would have to be escorted to Kyoto by his sponsor against hostile enemies on the way and as yet unknown armed opposition in the capital, so it was a huge gamble for both of them. Nobunaga expected that he could march peacefully from Owari through northern Ōmi because it was ruled by the Azai under the now retired Azai Hisamasa (1524–1573) and his son Nagamasa (1545–1573), who had helpfully become Nobunaga's brother-in-law. Just as in the case of Nobunaga's own marriage to Saitō Dōsan's daughter, his sister Oichi (1547–1583) had become a hostage by marriage. Oichi is perhaps the most famous wedded pawn in Japanese history, and her liaison with Azai Nagamasa would be just the beginning of a tumultuous and very sad adult life. They married either late in 1567 or early in 1568 and thereby guaranteed Nobunaga safe conduct.

Rokkaku Jōtei of Ōmi province, whose intransigence frustrated Nobunaga's advance against Kyoto in 1568. (ETKK 1855)

By contrast, in hostile southern Ōmi, Nobunaga would have to face the distinctly unsympathetic Rokkaku Jōtei. A week-long set of negotiations, during which Jōtei was promised the position of governor of Kyoto, failed to persuade him to acquiesce. Instead, he publicly declared his support for the rival shogun, Ashikaga Yoshihide, the child nominee of the Miyoshi faction who had finally been proclaimed shogun in the absence of the fugitive Yoshiaki. With no safe conduct promised, Oda Nobunaga responded in force by simply marching through northern Ōmi and invading southern Ōmi. Kannonji castle soon fell, and, over the next month, Nobunaga's armies crushed all other opposition.[5] The young shogun Yoshihide was killed during the course of the operation, and his sponsors Miyoshi and Matsunaga were forced to pay homage to Nobunaga. With all opposition eliminated, Nobunaga marched into Kyoto on 7 November 1568, where his very own nominee, Yoshiaki, was installed as the fifteenth, and as it turned out last, Ashikaga shogun.[6] The Jesuit missionary Luis Fróis claimed that Nobunaga led an army of 60,000 men in the operation. It may be an exaggeration, but it is a far cry from the 800 he started out with at the beginning of his military career.[7]

Kannonji castle, seat of the Rokkaku, captured by Nobunaga during his advance on Kyoto in 1568. (EIG 1881)

---

5   SKK 1965, p.85.
6   Lamers, *Japonius Tyrannus*, pp.58–59.
7   Anon., *Cartas que os padres e irmãos da Companhia de Iesus escreuerão dos Reynos de Iapão & China aos da mesma Companhia da India, & Europa des do Anno de 1549 até o de 1580* (Em Euora: Manoel de Lyra, 1598), vol. 1, f. 251v.

## ODA NOBUNAGA: SAMURAI COMMANDER 1534–82

### Nobunaga's Military Organisation in the Late 1560s and Early 1570s

It is about the year 1570 that we come across a few more facts and figures about how Oda Nobunaga was organising his growing army. By the time of his march on Kyoto in 1568, the core of Nobunaga's *kashindan* (warrior band) consisted of his family and those who had joined him while he was achieving absolute power within his native province of Owari. As time went by, Nobunaga acquired sons of his own, who always performed with unquestionable loyalty. His heir was Oda Nobutada, who was born in 1557 and was destined to share in his father's tragic death in 1582. Nobunaga's next two sons were born to different mothers within 20 days of each other in 1558. Oda Nobukatsu (sometimes read as Nobuo; 1558–1630) is officially regarded as the elder of the two, and, like his brother Nobutaka (1558–1583), he would be sent for adoption to a family in Ise as part of Nobunaga's pacification of that province. They are therefore often referred to as Kanbe Nobutaka and Kitabatake Nobukatsu.

Nobunaga kept his family members directly accountable to himself, while delegating the command of his other vassals through the *karō*, of whom the most famous was Shibata Katsuie. There was also a unit known as the *kogai no jikishin*, an expression that literally means 'direct vassals brought up from childhood'. Some fell into this category because they had literally acted as *koshō* (pages or squires) to Nobunaga from their childhood; they tended to be the sons of senior retainers and were groomed for stardom within Nobunaga's court. *Koshō* developed a strong devotion to their masters and were far from being ceremonial servants as the European expression page may suggest. In effect, they were his close personal attendants off the battlefield as well as on it.

This unidentified helmet on display in Maruoka castle bears a *mon* (badge) that may be a later variant of the original 'sliced quince' design used by the Oda family.

Nobunaga's Horse Guards made up his élite armoured bodyguard. The corps was founded in 1555, and the members of the unit were chosen because of their military skills rather than any impressive family lineage or ancestry. In about 1568, Nobunaga selected 20 men to create two troops: the black *horo* unit and the red *horo* unit, so named from the colour of the *horo*, the ornamental cloak or cowl that they wore. The first Horse Guards were all men from Nobunaga's home province of Owari, and, as Nobunaga's career progressed, a select few were admitted from conquered territories such as Mino province. In 1575, Nobunaga transferred control of Owari and Mino to Nobutada and took up residence in his magnificent palace-castle of Azuchi, taking many of the Horse Guards with him. In the late 1570s and early 1580s, their numbers were swelled further by samurai from the central provinces, but they were always selected on the grounds of military merit and battlefield prowess. For the whole of this time and until his death in 1582, the Horse Guards were at Nobunaga's side, so we read in *Shinchō-Kō ki* for the year 1569 that the Horse Guards accompanied him on a particular visit to Kyoto.[8] It is, however, difficult to determine their total numerical strength. In 1568, we hear of 60 guardsmen living in Azuchi castle while their wives and children stayed behind, and, in 1582, Nobunaga is recorded as having distributed 500 pheasants among the Horse Guards.

In the *Shinchō-Kō ki* entry for 2 October 1568, we find a clear statement that Nobunaga's Horse Guards were not used solely for defensive purposes. Nobunaga was conducting a campaign against the Rokkaku family and attacked their stronghold of Mitsukuriyama castle. The decision to use his precious guardsmen to lead the assault caused surprise to others in his close retainer band, because 'The previous year [Nobunaga] had brought the large province of Mino under his control. Presumably, thought the men of Mino, on this present occasion he would have them serve as his vanguard, but he did not have such a plan for the Mino-shū, and had his Horse Guards attack Mitsukuriyama'.[9]

Of his most famous generals, Toyotomi Hideyoshi and Sassa Narimasa (1536–1588) came from beyond the Oda sphere of influence (Hideyoshi may even have fought against the Hōjō as a retainer of the Imagawa in 1554), and a few other outsiders joined this 'officer class' after 1560. One was the infamous Akechi Mitsuhide (1528–1582), who was to betray him in 1582. Like Mitsuhide, the other serious traitor, Araki Murashige (1535–1586), also came from the ranks of the shogun's officials serving under Ashikaga Yoshiaki. Looking ahead, we may also note the famous Christian daimyo Takayama Ukon (1552–1615) joining the Horse Guards. All these senior officers were given enormous delegated responsibility, and we will in fact see little of Nobunaga on the battlefield in a personal capacity beyond 1577. Instead, his victories (and a few defeats) were the result of the trust he placed in his generals, without whose sterling efforts neither Nobunaga's military career nor his reputation can be correctly assessed.

In June 1569, Luis Fróis visited Nobunaga and provided a pen portrait of him. It is quite long, but the following points are particularly relevant to the present study of Nobunaga as a military man. 'The King of Owari …' wrote Fróis:

> is given to military exercises … a mastery of stratagems … hardly or not at all mindful of the reprimands or advice of his subordinates, and is feared and venerated by all to the highest degree … he always

---

8   SKK 1965, p.99.
9   SKK 1965, p.85.

## ODA NOBUNAGA: SAMURAI COMMANDER 1534–82

Flags and devices of Oda Nobunaga. Note in particular the inclusion of the flag of the Nichiren (Lotus) Sect to which Nobunaga belonged. (EIG 1881, detail)

has two thousand pages or horse guards with him. His father was Lord of Owari Province, but he, through his huge energy, has conquered seventeen or eighteen provinces in the last four years.[10]

It is also about this time that we find references to Nobunaga's use of a recognisable system of battlefield heraldry. The source is, however, the later war tale *Shinchō ki*, and the wording is ambiguous, because the 'yellow silk' of the *nobori* banners could mean 'raw silk', so some illustrations based on the description (including the well-known Nagashino Screen) show white banners while others prefer a golden yellow. The motif on all of them is, however, a representation of a coin struck by the Yongle Emperor of the Ming dynasty. Some pictures show three coins, others just one, but the banners also bear a pendant with the motto of the Nichiren Sect to which Nobunaga belonged. Later sources suggest that he may have used a large individual banner with the Nichiren motto on it. Nobunaga also used a *mon* (badge) of a sliced quince and had his field headquarters identified by his *uma jirushi* (battle standard), which was a huge three-dimensional golden umbrella.[11]

---

10   *Cartas* 1598, vol. 1, f. 257v.
11   Takahashi Kenichi, *Hata Sashimono* (Tokyo: Akita Shoten, 1965), pp.67–69.

# 4

# Nobunaga and the Battle of Anegawa

The years immediately following Ashikaga Yoshiaki's installation as shogun saw Japan being ruled by what was effectively a dual power system: that of the shogun and that of Oda Nobunaga, and, to some extent, each complemented the other. Nobunaga had supplied Yoshiaki with the backing he had always needed for his reign, and, in return, Yoshiaki had been able to give Nobunaga the power base he had lacked within Kyoto. Yet the wily Nobunaga took great care to keep his distance and stay independent of the shogun's control, as would be illustrated by his refusal to accept an office under Yoshiaki, who had asked him to become deputy shogun. Perhaps he thought that Yoshiaki's reign would not last forever and that, when it ended, Oda Nobunaga would be the true power in the land?

For the time being, therefore, Nobunaga was content to control and placate the shogun as much as he could while facing other military challenges that would add further to his reputation, and most of the threats involved the safety of his borders. The first challenge came from the strategic province of Ise, which was immediately adjacent to Owari. Its fate may be covered briefly, because, after success on the battlefield, Nobunaga forced the adoption of two of his sons into the main ruling families. Central Ise was controlled by the Kanbe family, who acquired Oda Nobutaka as their new heir. The more formidable southern Ise had seen its own local version of the transition from *shugo* to daimyo in the shape of the Kitabatake family, a house of glorious pedigree who had made their name during the fourteenth century. Their hold on the province was now shaky, and, in 1569, Kitabatake Tomonori (1528–1576) revolted against his elder brother in an appalling act of filial disloyalty that gave Nobunaga a useful pretext to attack their castle of Ōkawachi.[1] He began by burning to the ground the town around it and sealing off the fortress using bamboo palisades. Nobunaga's men

---

1   Lamers, *Japonius Tyrannus*, p.68.

patrolled the area between the multiple sets of fences, making sure that no one could leave. The first direct attack on Ōkawachi began under cover of darkness, but it started to rain, thereby making their firearms useless. The ensuing battle was a fierce hand-to-hand struggle, and 20 of Nobunaga's high-ranking samurai were killed, including two of his Horse Guards, along with about 300 other ranks. Greatly frustrated, Nobunaga scorched the surrounding area with the aim of starving the defenders to death, and, when the siege had lasted 50 days, Kitabatake proposed peace terms that included the adoption of Nobunaga's second son as his heir. This was agreed, and the eleven-year-old child was named Kitabatake Nobukatsu (1558–1630).[2] The only anti-Nobunaga elements now left within Ise were the *ikki* of the Nagashima delta. They would, however, prove to be as troublesome as any daimyo, as will be explained later.

## The First Echizen Campaign

Asakura Yoshikage, who defended Echizen province against Nobunaga for many years. This hanging scroll portrait of him is in Nagahama Castle Museum.

The Kitabatake may have put up a good fight before being completely neutralised, but other daimyo provided longer-lasting resistance to the Oda takeover, and the next few years of Nobunaga's military career would be dominated by the names of Asakura and Azai. These two daimyo lineages would set the pace of the anti-Nobunaga resistance until their gilded heads

---

2   SKK 1965, pp.96–99.

appeared at Nobunaga's banquet in 1574. The most important of them was Asakura Yoshikage (1533–1573), who ruled Echizen province from 1546 until his death in 1573. He had succeeded to the clan headship at the age of 15 and proved to be an accomplished warrior and administrator, having been blooded in war against the Ikkō Ikki, about whom we will have more to say in the chapter that follows. Otherwise, his early reign was largely peaceful, and Yoshikage was able to develop extensive trade from his elegant capital of Ichijōdani to areas as far away as Kyushu.

A superbly restored street section of the castle town of Ichijōdani, headquarters of the Asakura, which was completely destroyed by Nobunaga in 1573.

The outside world burst in upon peaceful Ichijōdani in 1566 in the person of the fugitive Ashikaga Yoshiaki. He stayed in the port of Tsuruga for over a year and was then found accommodation in a temple adjacent to Ichijōdani. Yoshiaki was treated royally, as befitted his rank, and his time with the Asakura shows the trust that each placed in the other. Yet that was where the relationship ended, because Yoshikage was not willing to risk everything by marching on Kyoto and installing Yoshiaki as the rightful shogun. That tremendous task, of course, would eventually be left to Nobunaga to accomplish, but, after his accession, Yoshiaki maintained cordial relations with the Asakura, and, when he was properly established as shogun, Yoshiaki sent a request to Asakura Yoshikage to come to Kyoto and serve in a position of responsibility. Suspecting a trap hatched by Nobunaga, Yoshikage declined. Yoshikage regarded Nobunaga as an upstart, albeit a very clever one who might try to capture Echizen in his absence. Much better service to the shogun could be performed, he reasoned, by the Asakura resisting Nobunaga, and quite a few other names of a similar persuasion were being tossed about. That was the start of the first anti-Nobunaga coalition, which Yoshiaki saw as a promising development, but, from Nobunaga's point of view, the refusal of the Asakura to visit the shogun

## ODA NOBUNAGA: SAMURAI COMMANDER 1534–82

gave him the pretext he needed to attack Yoshikage's Echizen province and expand his influence north of Kyoto.

Nobunaga's preparations for an invasion of Echizen began during the spring of 1570, although there is some confusion in the sources as to whether Echizen was his primary objective, because one version has Nobunaga setting out for Wakasa province to punish its daimyo, Mutō Tomoyasu, for rebelling against Yoshiaki. The account goes on to say that it was only when Asakura Yoshikage got involved in the Wakasa dispute that Nobunaga turned his attentions to Echizen.[3] The whole Wakasa affair could of course have been a feint, but the Asakura had already taken suitable precautions, enhancing their frontier defences around Tsuruga (which would be the area that he would enter first) and building new strongpoints along a line towards their capital.

The Asakura's frontier defence was centred on Tezutsuyama and Kanegasaki castles, which made up a combined fortification system along a single mountain ridge. Nobunaga first captured Tezutsuyama on 29 May 1570 and took 1,370 heads. When he moved on to Kanegasaki, the defence collapsed after some initial fighting, as would also happen also at nearby

Nobunaga's troops attack the Asakura fortress of Tezutsuyama and use wooden shields against a barrage of arrows and rocks. (ESSK 1803)

---

3    CLN 2011, p.142.

# NOBUNAGA AND THE BATTLE OF ANEGAWA

Hikida castle, which Nobunaga ordered to be demolished. With that, the frontier fortresses of Echizen had been completely neutralised. All that Nobunaga now had to do was to cross the highly defensible Kinome Pass, and the heartlands of Echizen province would be lying wide open to him, but, just as he was about to proceed onwards and attack Ichijōdani, Nobunaga received some very alarming news. His brother-in-law Azai Nagamasa had turned traitor and allied himself with the Asakura, thus cutting Nobunaga off from his most direct return route to Kyoto.

At first, Nobunaga dismissed the report as a wild rumour. It was soon confirmed, although a later legend credits his sister Oichi with warning Nobunaga of the defection. That is quite believable, because Oichi had been married off in Nobunaga's interests and may

The heroic defence of the castle of Kanegasaki against Nobunaga's army by Asakura samurai, who proudly display their names on their *sashimono* (back flags). (ETK 1799, detail)

well have provided the intelligence, but soon Nobunaga was forced into a retreat. A withdrawal, even a fighting withdrawal, was not something to which Oda Nobunaga would ever become accustomed, but he was determined not to let the evacuation of Echizen be turned into a rout. He had to avoid enemy troops, and the whole of Ōmi south of Lake Biwa was now hostile territory. Nobunaga therefore had to make his way round the less familiar northwestern shore of the lake guided by local sympathisers, thus avoiding any confrontation with Rokkaku Jōtei or Azai Nagamasa. The key local Oda sympathiser in the area turned out to be Kutsuki Mototsuna (1549–1632), who provided assistance for Nobunaga so that he was able to approach Kyoto via Ohara to the north of the capital.

Nobunaga's army was a large one, and its progress was slow, so Tokugawa Ieyasu and Toyotomi Hideyoshi were given the task of providing a fighting rearguard. Both of them accomplished that duty in a very distinguished manner, each covering the other as they fought their way out of Echizen. On one occasion, Hideyoshi's army were particularly hard pressed, at which the Tokugawa came over to assist them and Ieyasu did notable personal execution with a harquebus. Another of the Tokugawa heroes that day was Watanabe Hanzō Mōritsuna, who lived up to his nickname of 'Hanzō the

# ODA NOBUNAGA: SAMURAI COMMANDER 1534–82

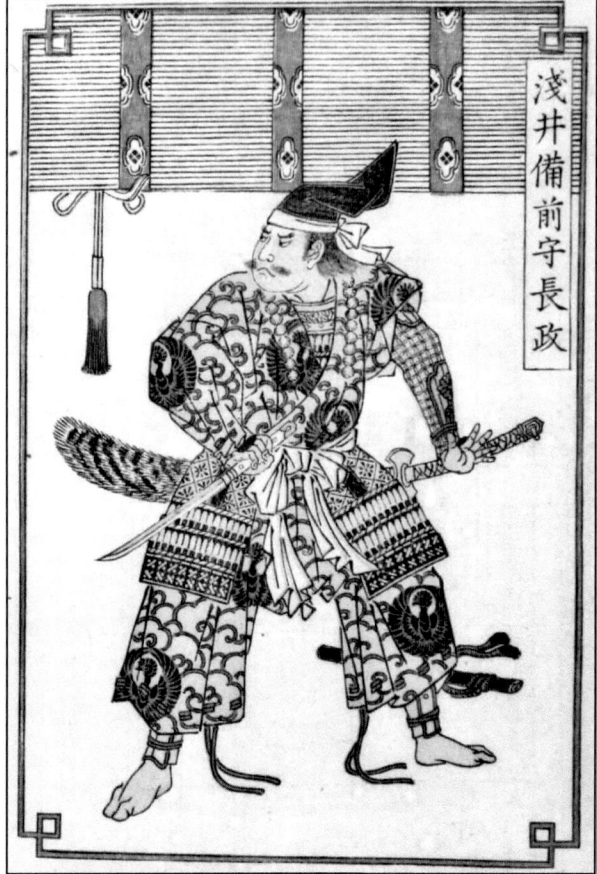

Azai Nagamasa, who became Nobunaga's brother-in-law but then abandoned him in favour of an ultimately disastrous alliance with Asakura Yoshikage. (EIG 1881)

Spear' when he cut down no less than 10 opponents using his *yari*.[4] The two armies then made their way back to Kyoto, where Nobunaga was already safely ensconced. On the way, Nobunaga had settled the matter of the rebellious lord of Wakasa by taking his mother hostage and destroying his castle, so the withdrawal was no hasty panic, thanks largely to Hideyoshi and Ieyasu.[5]

On returning to Kyoto, Nobunaga considered his next move. The defection of Azai Nagamasa had strengthened the growing anti-Nobunaga league, the members of whom were spread out around Nobunaga's key lines of communication between Gifu and Kyoto. Southern Ōmi had of course theoretically been pacified when Nobunaga marched through on his way to Kyoto in 1568, but, following their shock defeat, Rokkaku Jōtei and his son had taken refuge on the holy mountain of Kōyasan.[6] Having been unable to prevent Nobunaga's march on Kyoto, they were determined to make life as uncomfortable for him as possible in a largely guerrilla war that is illustrated by a number of key incidents when Nobunaga was making his way on campaign in one direction or the other. For example, 22 June 1570 found Nobunaga crossing the Chigusa Pass on his way back to Gifu, where a bold attempt was made on his life by a monk called Sugitani Zenjūbō, who was obviously a crack shot. He lay in wait for Nobunaga and fired two bullets at him (the account states that he had fired two bullets out of the same barrel), but both missiles merely grazed their noble victim, and he 'escaped from the jaws of the crocodile'. According to *Shinchō-Kō ki*, the man had been hired by Rokkaku Jōtei.[7] *Mikawa Go Fudoki* contains the same story, noting that 'two bullets came flying out of the dense forest' and hit Nobunaga's sleeve. He kept perfectly still while his attendants searched for the sniper.[8] The failed assassin Zenjūbō met a horrible death three years later, because he was apprehended by Nobunaga's men and interrogated about how he had managed to launch his ambush. Zenjūbō was then executed 'in a way Nobunaga had specially

---

4   KMGF 1976, vol. 1, p.369.
5   CLN 2011, p.143.
6   KMGF 1976, vol. 1, p.309.
7   SKK 1965, p.104.
8   KMGF 1886, pp.473–74.

# NOBUNAGA AND THE BATTLE OF ANEGAWA

designed. He was buried upright to his shoulders, and then his head was sawn off. Everyone, high and low, was very satisfied with this punishment'.[9]

Another anti-Nobunaga incident from around the same time brings us a famous anecdote about one of Nobunaga's most loyal generals: Shibata Katsuie, who had been given charge of Chōkōji castle when it was taken from the Rokkaku in 1568. Rokkaku Jōtei knew that the castle's only water supply came from some distance away and was conveyed by a succession of flimsy aqueducts. He soon succeeded in cutting off the water channels and waited until the garrison would suffer from thirst and had to surrender, but the castle showed no signs of weakening. Somewhat puzzled by this, Jōtei sent a messenger in the guise of a peace envoy, who asked for water while he was visiting. An attendant came out with water, and, after the envoy had washed his hands, he threw the remains away, so the messenger reported back to Jōtei that the garrison still had large supplies of water. That was of course not true; in fact, all they had left was contained in a few large earthenware jars. Katsuie was determined to go bravely to his death instead of dying of thirst within the fortress, so he shared the last of the water with his men and then smashed the water jars using his butt end of his *naginata*. He led his army out in what was intended to be a final suicidal charge, but so fierce was their assault that the Rokkaku army collapsed and Chōkōji was saved.[10]

Shibata Katsuie leads a desperate but ultimately successful sally out of besieged Chōkōji castle. (EIG 1881, detail)

---

9   SKK 1965, p.150.
10  As related in Yuasa Jōzan, *Jōzan Kidan* (Tokyo: Yohodo, 1912), <https://archive.org/details/jozankidan00yuasuoft/page/766/mode/2up>, p.88, accessed 31 May 2024.

# ODA NOBUNAGA: SAMURAI COMMANDER 1534–82

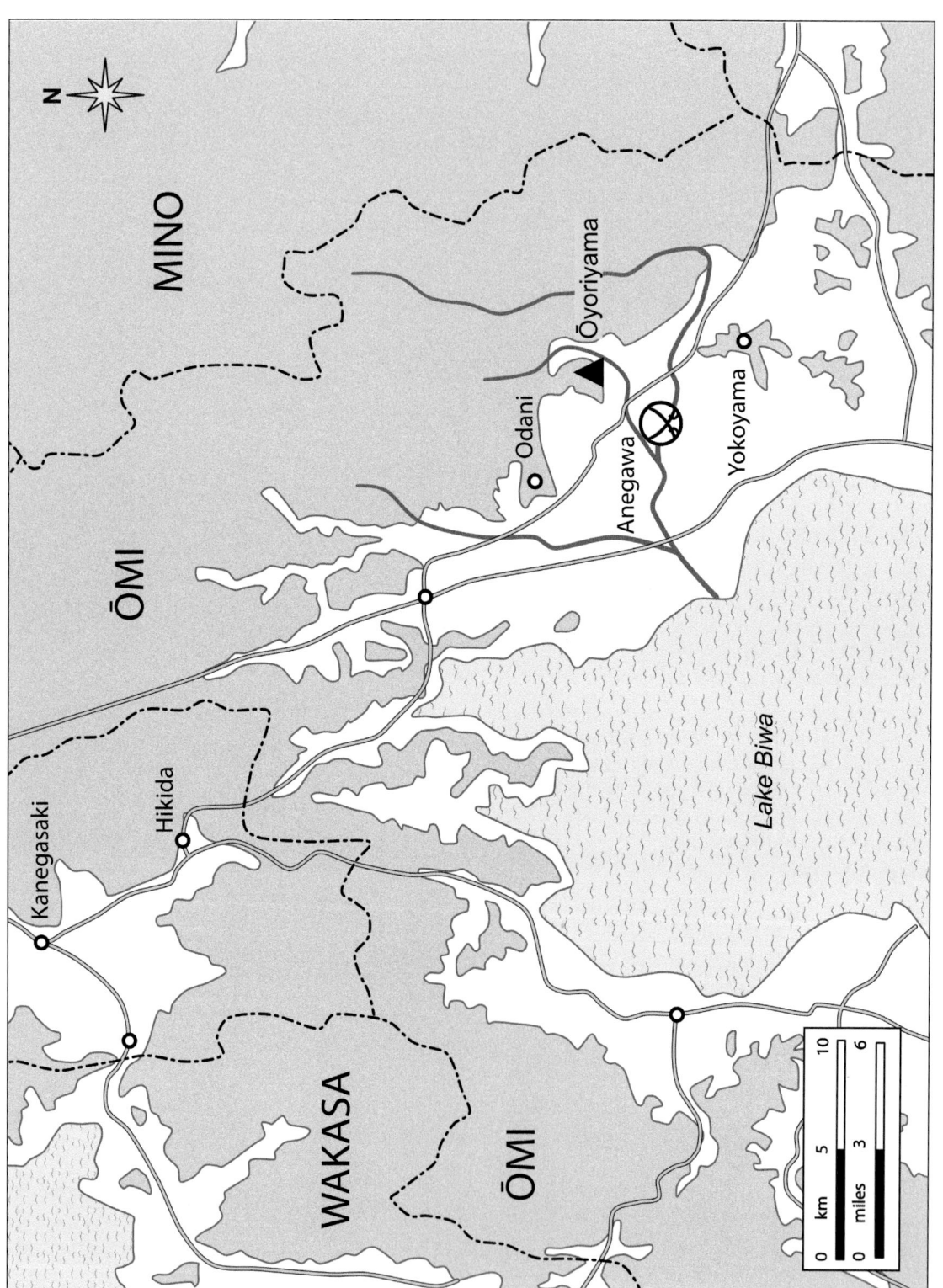

Nobunaga's wars against the Asakura and Azai, 1570–1573

# NOBUNAGA AND THE BATTLE OF ANEGAWA

## The Battle of Anegawa

In 1570, Nobunaga moved directly against the Azai and Asakura in a campaign that would be dominated by his famous victory at the battle of Anegawa (the Ane River). It is one of the battles that helped make his name, but, as my account will show, it was far from being a decisive encounter. In spite of very many casualties on his enemies' side, there was no thorough follow-up, and three more years would go by before the Asakura–Azai alliance was finally defeated. Nobunaga's victory also appears to have owed much to the fighting skills of his ally Tokugawa Ieyasu, although our main source for his involvement is admittedly the highly pro-Tokugawa *Mikawa Gofudo ki*.

In the months and days leading up to the battle of Anegawa, Asakura Yoshikage had cooperated with his allies in tit-for-tat raids against Nobunaga's positions in Mino and the repair of border castles in anticipation of an Oda advance against Azai positions in Ōmi. In mid-June, Nobunaga began by attacking his primary objective: Nagamasa's Odani castle, which was situated on a high mountain and was very well defended. Once again, Nobunaga tried the tactic of destroying the settlements round about, setting fire to all the villages as far as the last valley and backwater gully. Still the castle held, so Nobunaga withdrew on 24 July under cover of a rearguard supplied by Chūjō Ietada and Sassa Narimasa. A number of skirmishes took place at the foot of Odani to conceal Nobunaga's withdrawal, and several named samurai distinguished themselves in these actions. For example,

Sassa Narimasa, one of the loyal generals upon whom Nobunaga depended for his victories, seen here leading a charge around the time of the battle of Anegawa. One of his opponents wields the unusual weapon of a battle axe. (ESSK 1803)

Sassa Narimasa's unit deliberately 'drew the enemy towards themselves', while one of Chūjō's men 'managed to take his enemy's head at the bottom of the ditch, an exploit that earned him unparalleled fame'.[11]

Nobunaga's next moves can only be understood with reference to the local geography, because to the southeast of Odani was another important Azai fortress called Yokoyama and almost mid-way between Odani and Yokoyama lay a watery dividing line in the form of the Anegawa, which flowed westwards to enter Lake Biwa. When Nobunaga returned to the fray, he was joined by Tokugawa Ieyasu, and this time he directed his advance against Yokoyama castle as a secondary yet still very important objective, because it was vital that the link between Odani and Yokoyama was severed. He devastated the area around Odani and reckoned that its ruined state and the existence of the barrier of the Anegawa would leave his forces relatively undisturbed for their attack on Yokoyama.

However, it was the Asakura and Azai who set the pace, not Nobunaga, because Nobunaga's reinforcements from the Tokugawa would be matched by reinforcements sent from the Asakura. On being advised that Nobunaga had withdrawn from Odani, Yoshikage's commander in the field, Asakura Kagetake (1536–1575), advanced at the head of 8,000 men to take Nobunaga in the rear and set up lines on a mountain ridge called Ōyoriyama to the east of Odani. He was joined there by Azai Nagamasa, who made their allied force up to 13,000. From Ōyoriyama, they taunted Nobunaga and then tricked him by appearing to withdraw at dawn on 29 July. That encouraged Nobunaga to continue his siege of Yokoyama castle, but, at daybreak 24 hours later, they reappeared and marched down to the villages of Mitamura and Nomura, where they set up new positions with the Anegawa in front of them.[12]

The allied manoeuvring was an attempt to force Nobunaga to abandon Yokoyama and face them in battle across the river with the Yokoyama garrison still intact at his rear. Some commentators have used the words 'surprise attack' for the Azai–Asakura gambit, thus making a comparison with Nobunaga's assault at Okehazama. Pro-Nobunaga writers instead praise him for luring Azai Nagamasa out of Odani on to ground of his own choosing where the superior numbers of the Oda–Tokugawa army could be successfully deployed. So what really happened across the shallow waters of the Anegawa?

Whatever the plans, and whoever was the surprised party, the two rivals had both left any protection that castles or fortified field positions could have provided and were now facing each other across a wide river early on a summer's morning. Tokugawa Ieyasu had brought 6,000 men to join Nobunaga's 23,000. He may have wished to bring more, but Ieyasu was facing a challenge from Takeda Shingen and needed to keep his own castles fully manned. Nobunaga therefore had the advantage of numbers, but some of his troops were of doubtful reliability because they had been levied for

---

11   CLN 2011, pp.146–47.
12   CLN 2011, p.147.

service from lands that had previously belonged to the Azai. The brilliant Toyotomi Hideyoshi was put in charge of this questionable contingent, and Nobunaga was so confident of victory that he was not wearing armour, only a light summer *kimono* under a black *haori* jacket, and with no head protection other than a lightweight foot soldier's *jingasa*.

To some extent, the overall layout of the battlefield and the shared command ensured that the Oda and Tokugawa armies operated almost independently of each other, although there is a tradition that, before the battle, Ieyasu pleaded with Nobunaga to be given command of the vanguard. When Nobunaga refused, claiming not unreasonably that his dispositions were already settled and that to reorganise his army now would cause problems, Ieyasu threatened to withdraw his troops. Alternatively, Nobunaga is said to have asked Ieyasu to fight the Asakura contingent because Nobunaga wanted to settle the personal grudge he had with his treacherous brother-in-law Nagamasa.[13] Whatever arguments may have occurred, in the final layout, the Oda headquarters unit lay to the rear, with the rest of his army spread along the riverbank. The Tokugawa held the left flank, directly across the Anegawa from the Asakura troops, and the Asai and Asakura contingents were arranged in five and four ranks deep, respectively. Nobunaga arranged his own army 13 ranks deep to absorb the impact of a charge, and events would prove that this was a sensible decision, because the Azai–Asakura army would give him a very hard time. If the Asakura–Azai alliance had a plan at all, it was likely to have been that the Azai should hold the Oda forces while the main Asakura army tried to destroy the numerically inferior Tokugawa.

According to *Shinchō-Kō ki*, the fight began at 6:00 a.m. and was a 'terrible, confused, man-to-man battle'.[14] The first move was made by the Azai, who entered the river to attack Nobunaga's left flank. As it was summer, the sky was already light, and, as the day wore on, the sun climbed higher and blazed down onto the two armies. There appears to be little evidence of tactical precision on either side; instead, the overall impression is of a huge melee conducted with great violence in the middle of the shallow river. *Shinchō-Kō ki* provides very few details of the action other than to claim that Nobunaga finally 'crushed the enemy' and to give a list of notable heads,[15] so we have to look elsewhere to get a feel of the battle. *Mikawa Gofudo ki* naturally emphasises the achievements of the Mikawa men under Ieyasu, and, at first, it was almost as though there were two separate battles being fought: the Tokugawa against the Asakura, and the Oda upstream against the Asai. Both armies waded into the river, which flowed slowly and was about one metre deep at the most. The sweat poured off the samurai and their horses to mingle with the waters of the river, which were soon stained red as arrows and bullets found their mark.

---

13     KMGF 1976, vol. 1, p.376.
14     CLN 2011, p.147.
15     CLN 2011, p.148.

This illustration of the battle of Anegawa in 1570 pits Isono Kazumasa against Nobunaga's general Sakuma Nobumori. (EIG 1881)

Anegawa is not usually cited as an example of Nobunaga's grasp of firearms technology, although there are two references in *Shinchō-Kō ki* that confirm his use of large numbers of guns. The first states that, the day before the battle, Nobunaga deployed 500 harquebuses in his rearguard alone when he withdrew from Odani and, when the battle of Anegawa was at its height, there were 'clouds of black smoke'.[16] *Mikawa Gofudo ki* also states that Tokugawa Ieyasu opened his attack with bows and guns.[17] Yet Anegawa was not Nagashino. The harquebuses at Anegawa may have been deployed in large numbers, but their operators were not firing from behind field fortifications but across (and even within) a river, which was not an ideal situation for gunpowder weapons. However, anecdotal evidence concerning two of the heroes of Anegawa points to the extensive use of firearms by both sides. The first concerns Isono Kazumasa, who was the keeper of Sawayama castle in Ōmi on behalf of Azai Nagamasa. At Anegawa, he led his unit directly against Nobunaga and blasted the Oda vanguard of 2,000 men with a volley of gunfire before emerging out of the smoke with a spear in his hands.[18] Heroic though Isono's attack may have been, it was effectively

---

16  SKK 1965, pp.106–07.
17  KMGF 1976, vol. 1, p.377.
18  Elena Varshavskaya, *Heroes of the Grand Pacification* (Amsterdam: Hotei

# NOBUNAGA AND THE BATTLE OF ANEGAWA

wasted. Among those caught in his bombardment was the 15-year-old Sakai Kyūzō, a retainer of Oda Nobunaga. On recovering from the assault, Kyūzō led 50 men in an attack on Azai Nagamasa's field headquarters. He killed dozens of men with his spear and was approaching Nagamasa himself when he became the target of concentrated harquebus fire from over a hundred of Nagamasa's bodyguard. Kyūzō was hit by four bullets and died instantly.[19]

When the Tokugawa launched their first attack with bows and guns, the Asakura commander observed the action and came to the conclusion that the enemy were a small force who could quickly be eliminated. He therefore ordered into action some warrior monks from the Heisenji of Echizen province. The Heisenji was a powerful institution on a par with the Asakura themselves, although so many of its adherents were Asakura vassals that they were natural allies rather than rivals. The loyal monks began to drive back the Tokugawa army. Ieyasu's men had clearly been taken by surprise, but they rallied under the command of one of the most famous of all the Mikawa leaders: Honda Tadakatsu (1548–1610), who 'suddenly sprinted his horse and broke through the enemy like lightning'. *Mikawa Gofudo ki* sums up the action as follows:

Fifteen-year-old Sakai Kyūzō, a retainer of Oda Nobunaga, was killed by concentrated harquebus fire at Anegawa. His death is circumstantial evidence for the extensive deployment of firearms at that famous battle.

> Ieyasu ordered Sakakibara [Yasumasa] and Honda Bungo-no-Kami [Tadakatsu] to attack the enemy in the flank. Yasumasa looked back. In front [the river] was shallow with sand and stones on the bottom like a paddy field. Seeing him ride his horse into it Bungo-no-Kami … similarly advanced and engaged in battle. Abe Tadamasa repeatedly loosed his bow at the enemy.[20]

---

Publishing, 2005), pp.78–79.
19  Varshavskaya, *Heroes*, pp.82–83.
20  KMGF 1976, vol. 1, p.377.

## ODA NOBUNAGA: SAMURAI COMMANDER 1534–82

The most celebrated individual hero of the battle of Anegawa was Magara Jurōzaemon Naotaka, who single-handedly protected the Asakura retreat across the river. His preferred weapon was a long-bladed ōdachi. (ETK 1799)

Other Mikawa heroics followed, including some vigorous fighting by Naitō Masasada, who was so engrossed that he dropped his spear and had to return to retrieve it after a brief retreat. Matsui Sakon was hit in the left hand by an arrow that went through into the front pommel of his saddle, but (in a version of a popular samurai trope) he pulled out his arrow and used it to fell his enemy.

The repulse of the Asakura advance by the men of Mikawa was a decisive moment in the battle, because Honda Tadakatsu's counterattack had been so successful that Asakura Kagetake was now completely surrounded in the middle of the river. It was essential that the Asakura army withdrew to the protection of the northern bank, and a retainer of the Asakura called Magara Jurōzaemon Naotaka volunteered to cover their retreat. Magara was a giant of a man, whose preferred weapon was not a spear but the longer version of the ordinary *tachi* known as an *ōdachi* or *nodachi*. The actual length of Magara's *ōdachi* depends on which version of the story one reads. The usual length given is five *shaku* three *sun* (160.6 centimetres), which is large enough for a blade for practical use. The *Mikawa Go Fudoki* makes no reference to the length of the weapon, but other accounts have it down as six *shaku* (181.8 centimetres) or even an unlikely seven *shaku* eight *sun* (236.3 centimetres).[21]

---

21    Suzuki Masaya, *Katana to kubotori* (Tokyo: Heibonsha, 2000), p.128.

**Plate A. Oda Nobunaga at the head of his army c. 1573.**
*See Colour plates commentary for further information.*

Plate B. A life-sized diorama formerly on display at Kiyosu castle, showing Oda Nobunaga performing a chant from a Noh play.
*See Colour plates commentary for further information.*

**Plate C. The death of Imagawa Yoshimoto at the battle of Okehazama.**
*See Colour plates commentary for further information.*

**Plate D. The army of Asakura Yoshikage.**
*See Colour plates commentary for further information.*

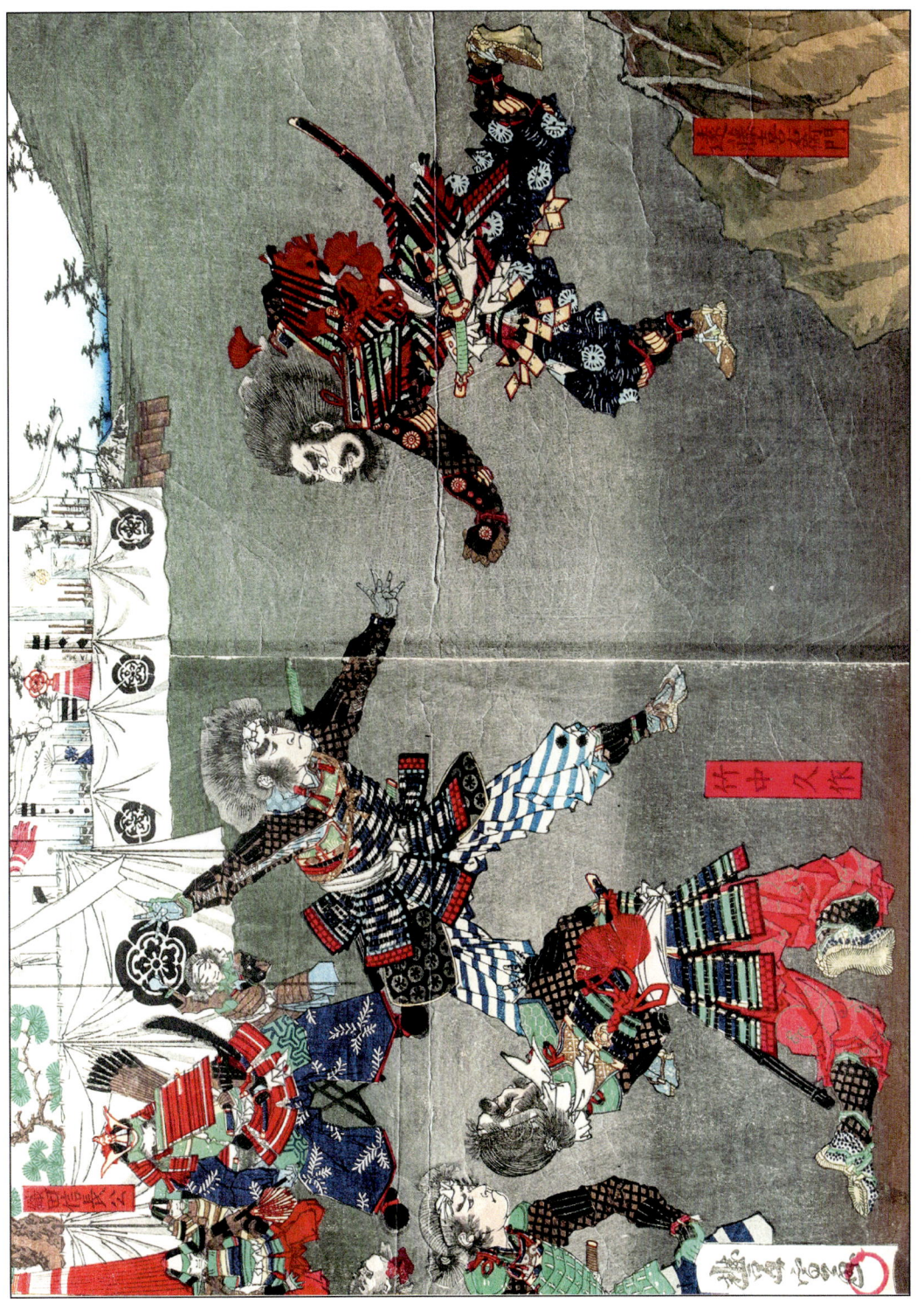

**Plate E. Endō Naotsugu at the battle of Anegawa.**
*See Colour plates commentary for further information.*

**Plate F. A modern golden statue of Nobunaga.**
*See Colour plates commentary for further information.*

**Plate G. An armour of *dō-maru* style**
*See Colour plates commentary for further information.*

**Plate H. The hero Mori Yoshinari (1523-70).**
*See Colour plates commentary for further information.*

**Plate I. The restored outer gateway of the Asakura mansion of Ichijōdani.**
*See Colour plates commentary for further information.*

**Plate J. A modern interpretation of the banner showing the crucified Torii Sune'emon.**
*See Colour plates commentary for further information.*

**Plate K. This is claimed to be the actual helmet worn by Nobunaga at the battle of Nagashino.**
*See Colour plates commentary for further information.*

**Plate L. Oda Nobunaga at the battle of Nagashino in 1575.**
*See Colour plates commentary for further information.*

**Plate M. The battle of Nagashino.**
*See Colour plates commentary for further information.*

**Plate N. A modern interpretation of of Nobunaga's multi-storeyed masterpiece of Azuchi castle.**
*See Colour plates commentary for further information.*

**Plate O. Akechi Mitsuhide.**
*See Colour plates commentary for further information.*

**Plate P. This armour is said to have belonged to Akechi Mitsuharu.**
*See Colour plates commentary for further information.*

**Plate Q. Oda (Kanbe) Nobutaka (1568-83).**
*See Colour plates commentary for further information.*

**Plate R. Oda Nobunaga.**
*See Colour plates commentary for further information.*

# NOBUNAGA AND THE BATTLE OF ANEGAWA

Like the samurai of old, whose stories he would have been told as a child, Magara issued a challenge to anyone from the Tokugawa side who would come to fight him. 'I am a person called Magara Jurōzaemon', he shouted in a loud voice. 'If anyone forgets it I shall show who I am by gaining my customary victory!' That was a good diversionary tactic to adopt at any time in samurai history, and Magara was not disappointed, because his challenge was first accepted by a warrior whom he killed. He was then joined by his eldest son, Magara Jurōsaburō Naomoto. Naomoto wielded a shorter *ōdachi* of four *shaku* three *sun* in length, and together father and son faced off repeated attacks by the Tokugawa samurai. Gradually, the Asakura army managed to disengage itself and pull back across the river as the two heroes followed slowly, swinging their huge weapons in wide circles and lopping off arms and legs.

It required a simultaneous attack by four samurai to defeat them, namely, the three brothers Kosaka Shikibu, Gorojirō and Rokurogorō plus their comrade Yamada Muneroku. Magara Jurōzaemon met the first named with some force and swung his enormous sword at him, which cut Kosaka Shikibu on the thigh, then with a second slash knocked the helmet off his head, smashing it to the ground. He then cut through Shikibu's spear. At this, Shikibu's younger brother ran to his assistance but was met by a vicious sweep to his side. Yamada Muneroku, a veteran warrior 60 years old, lost his weapon when his spear shaft parted under a blow from Magara, leaving the third brother to join in the fray. He was armed with a cross bladed spear and managed to hook one of the side blades under Magara's armour and haul him from his horse to the ground, at which Magara was quickly decapitated. His son tried to withdraw to the Asakura army while attempting to avenge his father but was met by a samurai who engaged him in fierce fighting, at the end of which the younger Magara was killed. Their sacrifice had not been in vain, because their rearguard action had allowed the army to rally, even though they were then pursued for a considerable distance.[22]

Another celebrated hero who fought on the Asakura–Azai side was Endō Naotsugu, whom *Mikawa Go Fudoki* credits with a plan to bring about a victory in one stroke. His idea was to infiltrate Nobunaga's bodyguards and then assassinate Nobunaga. To do this, he carefully removed any distinguishing insignia from his armour, dishevelled his hair, smeared his face with blood and picked up a severed head from the battlefield. His ploy was to pretend that he was presenting the head to Nobunaga. He got as far as Nobunaga's curtained headquarters but was apprehended by Takenaka Shigenori, at which Endō threw the severed head in Nobunaga's direction before he was cut down.[23]

The battle of Anegawa was resolved when Nobunaga's troops who were besieging Yokoyama risked leaving the siege lines, and Lamers provides a translation of Nobunaga's own report on the subsequent victory. He states

---

22  KMGF 1976, vol. 1, p.378.
23  Varshavskaya, *Heroes*, pp.84–85.

that his enemies 'advanced on a village called Nonamura in an effort to relieve Yokoyama' but does not acknowledge being taken unawares. As far as Nobunaga is concerned, 'We scored a great victory. As far as heads are concerned, I have no idea at the moment how many ... [but] the fields and paddies are covered with corpses'. He concludes with a mention of the disagreement over who should lead the first attack and says that Ieyasu was granted the honour, although there is no reference to Ieyasu threatening to walk away from the battlefield.[24] As for the heads, the total is precisely recorded in *Mikawa Go Fudoki* as 3,170, although it is likely that large numbers of troops on both sides never engaged because the front was so narrow, in which case the death toll would have been much higher.[25]

One mystery about the battle of Anegawa is why Nobunaga did not pursue his retreating and defeated enemy. It may be that he wished to persuade Azai Nagamasa back to his side, so for his men run to riot in northern Ōmi would not be in Nobunaga's best interests. Nevertheless, the decision not to follow up would cost him dearly in military terms because Nagamasa remained an enemy of the Azai and his allies the Asakura also survived to fight another day. Nobunaga did advance as far as Odani, but once again he found it very difficult to besiege, so he withdrew to Gifu to rest on his laurels. The Asakura's recovery was, however, both quick and considerable, because, within three months of the battle of Anegawa, Yoshikage felt able to challenge Nobunaga again along with new allies. Yoshikage's new associates were the Buddhist sectarians of the Ikkō Ikki, whose involvement would influence the entire course of Nobunaga's remaining career.

---

24   Lamers, *Japonius Tyrannus*, pp.48–49.
25   KMGF 1886, pp.481–82.

# 5

# Nobunaga and the Ikkō Ikki

From about the time of the battle of Anegawa onwards, much of Nobunaga's military activity was conducted to a background of a long series of bitter campaigns against certain armies who embraced Buddhist sectarian beliefs as part of their collective identity. The most powerful among them, an organisation known as the Ikkō Ikki (the single-minded league), would become early partners in the anti-Nobunaga coalition, and the 'Ishiyama War' (as their contribution to the struggle against him would become known from the name of their headquarters) was destined to last on and off for 10 years. The Ikkō Ikki's first operations were intertwined with the events related in the previous chapter and would continue to influence Nobunaga's plans and achievements right up until the moment of his death.

## Buddhist Armies as Enemies and Allies

So far, we have seen armed resistance to Oda Nobunaga being conducted largely by people like him: daimyo or those who aspired to that rank, but he had other enemies too, whose opposition to Oda Nobunaga and other warlords was in some ways a class war. That was because the 'top down' social model on which the daimyo depended was not the only possibility for contemporary governance that had arisen out of the breakdown of central authority following the Ōnin War. In other situations, local *kokujin* ('provincial men' or small landholders) and *jizamurai* (part-time samurai/farmers) formed *ikki* (confederacies or leagues). *Ikki* took many forms but were typically voluntary organisations brought into being on egalitarian lines by communities whose members shared common interests and had similar enemies. Communities like these resisted the vertical model of daimyo governance that had been developing for over a century in favour of a more horizontal one that tended towards a structure vaguely recognisable as democracy, although some *ikki* became as hierarchical as any daimyo. *Ikki* could also be very militant organisations, and, when it came to making war, they proved to be the equal of grander opponents. Nobunaga may have defeated daimyo like Imagawa and Saitō, but, throughout all of his career, he could not consider a province to have been pacified unless any local *ikki* had also been quelled, and quelled they had to be, because the status of subservient vassal was decidedly not to their taste.

It is, however, important to realise that the word '*ikki*' can have two meanings, because, when it is encountered in a historical narrative, it should sometimes be translated as 'riot' or 'uprising'. By the 1570s, some of these revolts had taken on an almost permanent form, transforming an *ikki* into a league, and highly prominent among the many groups whose allegiance took this shape were the Ikkō Ikki, whose Buddhist faith provided the unifying factor that held them together. Their name will feature prominently in the pages that follow, as it does in any history of sixteenth-century Japan. That familiarity has meant that the Ikkō Ikki are often regarded as the only *ikki* that existed, so it is important to note that other religious and non-religious *ikki* were active at the time and will play an important role in our story.

The Ikkō Ikki's personal allegiance was to a very narrow sectarian view of Buddhism, because their *monto* (followers or disciples) belonged to a particular branch of Jōdo Shinshū (The True Pure Land Sect) that went under the name of the Honganji (The Temple of the Original Vow). Its leader at the time of Nobunaga was the Patriarch Kennyo Kōsa (1543–1592), who would become an influential member of the anti-Nobunaga coalition. Some of his allies sympathised with the Honganji's creed; others merely shared an antipathy to Nobunaga. The Ikkō Ikki headquarters was a temple complex known to later history as Ishiyama Honganji, which was built across a series of islands in the river delta where Osaka castle now stands, yet, in spite of its adherents' close identification with a temple, it is highly misleading to refer to the Ikkō Ikki as warrior monks. Instead, the organisation attracted samurai, farmers and townsmen from both urban and rural communities.

It is not generally appreciated that Ishiyama Honganji had only a small standing army of its own but was willingly defended by sympathetic volunteers and was safely supplied by sea. The temple therefore fully justified the term 'impregnable', and it is remarkable to note that, during his 10-year-long campaign against the Ikkō Ikki, Oda Nobunaga never once attempted to attack Ishiyama Honganji directly. Nevertheless, because of an influence that was at the same time spiritual, economic and military, Ishiyama Honganji became a black hole in the galaxy that was Nobunaga's *tenka* (realm), and his campaigns against it encouraged the Honganji to label him as the foe of Buddhism itself. That may not have been strictly true, but it was certainly an opinion shared by the Jesuit missionaries whom Nobunaga favoured. Having met him in 1569, Luis Fróis believed that Nobunaga despised 'the *kami* (deities), the *hotoke* (Buddhas) and all types of idols and gentile superstition'.[1] Writing in 1582, Father Gaspar Coelho saw what Nobunaga had done to his sectarian enemies and noted that 'he is still a cruel enemy, and persecutor of the Bonzos (priests), and in his

---

1   *Cartas* 1598, vol. 1, f. 257v.

kingdom he has destroyed so many principal villages and killed so many Bonzos, and he discourages all of them so much, that their sects are already very dejected'.[2]

Unlike his rivals Uesugi Kenshin and Takeda Shingen, Nobunaga never entered holy orders by having his head shaved and taking a religious name, but he was not lacking in personal beliefs. He was in fact a member of the Lotus Sect that had been founded by the monk Nichiren and flew small pennants from the staffs of his banners that bore the Nichiren motto, 'Namu Myōhō Renge Kyō' (Devotion to the Mystic Law of the Lotus Sutra), a gesture that must have enraged the Ikkō Ikki all the more. He may also have used a large personal banner with the motto on it, because the war tale *Ishiyama Gunki* includes a story that is probably fictional but nevertheless suggests that Nobunaga had a genuine devotion to the sect. During a battle with the Ikkō Ikki in 1570, this large Nichiren flag was lost to the enemy. The following day, a young warrior by the name of Maeda Toshiie recaptured the banner and brought it back safely. It is interesting to see this tale being incorporated into a story that glorifies the Honganji, unless its purpose is further to denigrate Nobunaga by association with a despised rival sect.[3]

Ishiyama Honganji actively encouraged other *monto* in Ise, Ōmi, Echizen and Kaga towards acts of defiance against Nobunaga: operations that would earn the Ikkō Ikki the reputation of being death-defying religious fanatics who believed that death in battle assured them of a place in paradise. In fact, that idea conflicted with the teaching of the sect's founder, who had taught that rebirth in paradise depended on faith, not actions. Nevertheless, one of the slogans that would appear on their flags proclaimed that he who

An anecdotal story that appears in war tales about Oda Nobunaga relates how Maeda Toshiie recaptured Nobunaga's Nichiren flag from the Ikkō Ikki in 1570. (ESSK 1803)

---

2   Anon., *Segunda parte das cartas de Iapão que escreuerão os padres, & irmãos da companhia de Iesus* (Em Euora: Manoel de Lyra, 1598), vol. 2, f. 30r.
3   Okamoto Sensuke (ed.), *Ishiyama Gunki* (Tokyo: Igyō-kan, 1895), pp.145–47. The story also appears in Niwa Tōkei and Ryūkōsai Nyokei, *Ehon Shūi Shinchō ki* (Tokyo: Publisher unknown, 1803), vol. 5.

# ODA NOBUNAGA: SAMURAI COMMANDER 1534–82

*Monto* (disciples) of the Honganji heading off to war bearing simple straw matting banners on which the sacred Buddhist invocation 'Namu Amida Butsu' has been handwritten. (ESSK 1803)

advanced was sure of Heaven while he who retreated would suffer the torments of Hell.

The majority of these *monto* were the part-time warrior/farmers noted above, but many of their leaders were modestly wealthy men, for whom the European terms 'barons' or 'gentry' provide useful analogies. Their contribution ensured that Ikkō Ikki armies were never just a mob of rioting peasants, although some shared very humble origins and are authentically recorded as going into action armed with agricultural tools and weapons. That practice has led to another skewed image of them as merely poor farmers. It must, however, be pointed out that Oda Nobunaga (among other daimyo) regarded them in precisely that light, despising them as vermin to be exterminated and haughtily dismissing their fighting skills even when they defeated him in battle. Nobunaga was, however, a skilful manipulator of people. Other Jōdo Shinshū groups existed in addition to the Honganji faction, and that was a factor that he exploited on several occasions by using alliances and bribery to persuade them to join his own forces. Sometimes, the process was helped when his Buddhist opponents became their own worst enemies. That happened usually when the sect's other branches objected to the primacy assumed and exerted so vigorously by the aggressive Honganji faction, who tended to impose a very daimyo-like control.

To add to the complicated mix of non-daimyo organisations that existed during the Sengoku Period, there were also several groups of genuine warrior monks in existence, and the most important were the militant

Shingon sect followers from the temple complex of Negoroji in Kii province. Negoroji was a very rich establishment with huge landholdings that gave it an economic and political power comparable to that of a large daimyo.[4] Its adherents, too, were highly skilled in military matters and maintained an army of fighting men to defend their more piously inclined brethren. Negoroji was visited in 1571 by the Jesuit missionary Gaspar Vilela, who wrote of its inhabitants that 'some of them are usually at their prayers, others are engaged in the wars, and all of them are required to make five arrows every day and always to keep their weapons ready'.[5] That was hardly an exaggeration, but the great military asset that Negoroji possessed was an early embrace of firearms brought about through fortuitous personal connections and active trading partnerships. The Negoroji monks became so secure within their communities that they would sell their services to others as gun-toting mercenaries, and Nobunaga would become one of their most favoured clients. The nearby district of Saika in Kii was closely associated with both Negoroji and the Honganji and would also play a part in Nobunaga's wars.

## Nobunaga and the Honganji

The first contact that Nobunaga had with Ishiyama Honganji was made in 1567 and was a cordial one, but the peaceful interaction carried a hidden message. The background was that, when Nobunaga gained control of Mino and northern Ise, Kennyo Kōsa sent him a letter of congratulations and a gift of a sword. The meaning behind the present was that one ruler was congratulating another as an equal.[6] Nobunaga is unlikely to have been fooled by the gesture, and indeed the friendly mood changed in 1568. After entering Kyoto in triumph with Ashikaga Yoshiaki, Nobunaga placed a financial levy on a number of institutions, including Ishiyama Honganji. Seemingly cowed, Kennyo paid up, but, at the same time, he decided to oppose Nobunaga through the making of alliances with the Rokkaku, the Asakura–Azai, the Miyoshi and the Matsunaga. He also ordered the 10 Honganji temples in Ōmi province, whose close proximity to Nobunaga's sphere of influence made them key players, to prepare for an uprising, although they probably needed no prompting because Nobunaga had devastated their lands when he marched through hostile Ōmi province in 1568.[7]

It therefore came about that Nobunaga's battlefield introduction to the Ikkō Ikki happened not at Osaka but in Ōmi during the months leading

---

4 Owada Tetsuo, *Hideyoshi no tenka tōitsu sensō* (Tokyo: Yoshikawa Kobunkan, 2006), p.152.
5 *Cartas* 1598, vol. 1, f. 114v.
6 McMullin, *Buddhism*, p.102.
7 McMullin, *Buddhism*, p.103.

## ODA NOBUNAGA: SAMURAI COMMANDER 1534–82

up to the battle of Anegawa. *Shinchō-Kō ki* tells us that the *ikki* rose up sometime around the beginning of June 1570 and burned villages under Nobunaga's control. On 6 July, in conjunction with sympathisers from the adjacent Iga province, they moved down the Yasugawa under the leadership of Rokkaku Jōtei but were intercepted by Nobunaga's army under Shibata Katsuie and Sakuma Morimasa (1554–1583) at the village of Ochikubo, where '780 of the finest samurai from the Iga and Kōka-shū' were killed.[8] The Ōmi *ikki* also put in an appearance in the aftermath of the battle of Anegawa of behalf of the Asakura, whose astonishing recovery made it look as though that famous fight across the river had never happened. Having formulated an alliance with the Honganji, Asakura Yoshikage sent his army into Ōmi to link up with Azai Nagamasa and the local Ikkō Ikki to make up an army of 30,000 men to fight Nobunaga again, and all this was in place within three months of Anegawa!

The allies' strategy from that point onwards was an incredibly bold one, because they intended to enter Kyoto and reverse Nobunaga's achievement of installing his own nominee as shogun, and their attack was planned to begin while Nobunaga was engaged elsewhere. That is where the Ishiyama Honganji *monto* first enter the story, because Nobunaga was already fighting them in the Osaka area, even though they had not been his primary objective. Nobunaga's targets when he began the Osaka campaign were the three regents of the Miyoshi clan (their leader was still a minor) who were known collectively as the Miyoshi Sanninshū (the Miyoshi 'three-man force' or 'Triumvirs'). Having been driven from Kyoto a few years earlier, they had scurried back to their ancestral lands in Awa province on Shikoku, but, by 1570, they felt strong enough to return and take up the fight against Nobunaga. The Miyoshi, who had been joined by pirates from Awaji island, crossed from Shikoku to Settsu province and set up positions at the two forts of Noda and Fukushima, defended by 8,000 men. The outposts lay not far to the north of Ishiyama

The Miyoshi army awaits Nobunaga's attack upon the fortress of Noda. (EIG 1881)

---

8  SKK 1965, pp.103–04.

## NOBUNAGA AND THE IKKŌ IKKI

Honganji, with whom the Triumvirs maintained a friendly and supportive understanding against Nobunaga.

Bolstered by his victory at the battle of Anegawa, Nobunaga decided to take the fight directly to the Miyoshi, and, on 25 September 1570, he began his attack on the two forts. The *Shinchō-Kō ki* account of the 1570 campaign is, however, highly revealing about Nobunaga's firearms capacity because of the contrast Ōta Gyūichi draws between Nobunaga's own arsenal and the contribution he received from supposedly 20,000 warrior monks from Negoroji and mercenaries from elsewhere in Kii province. The visitors were said to have 3,000 harquebuses, so 'the thunder of friendly and of enemy guns made heaven and earth shake night and day'.[9] The figure quoted here for his Kii allies is more likely to be the total number of their communities who lived in the province, which included men, women and children, and the number of guns may also have been much less than 3,000.[10] Whatever the correct army size might be, the extensive firing and counter-firing at Noda and Fukushima probably represents the first large-scale gunfight in the history of Japanese warfare.[11] As for Nobunaga's personal contribution to the bombardment, the impression given in *Shinchō-Kō ki* is that the number of his allies' guns dwarfed those of Nobunaga's own, and of course the expression 'enemy guns' confirms that the Miyoshi had lots of them too. All of this stands in contrast to the popular image of Nobunaga as Japan's great innovator in firearms use.

When the two sides engaged, there was some defection from the Miyoshi to Nobunaga's side, after which Nobunaga advanced his headquarters to Tenmagamori, which lay on the same island as the other two forts. From there, he sent out numerous soldiers to cut grass and reeds to make bundles that would be dropped into the inlets and ditches

The army of Oda Nobunaga, identified by the Oda *mon* that appears on their jackets. The character on the left carrying a harquebus could be one of the firearms mercenaries from Negoroji whom Nobunaga employed on a regular basis. (ESSK 1803, detail)

---

9   SKK 1965, p.110.
10  McMullin, *Buddhism*, p.306.
11  Katsura Hidezumi, 'Ishiyama Honganji Kassen', *Rekishi Dokuhon*, 33:19 (1988), p.98.

Nobunaga continued his advance against Noda and Fukushima by moving his headquarters forward to Tenmagamori, which brought him close to Ishiyama Honganji. (EIG 1891)

to make causeways for the proposed attack on Noda and Fukushima. A few days later, Nobunaga set up another forward post to the west of the forts at a location called Ebie, where his men began building earthwork defences. When the assault was launched, each unit strove to outdo the others as they fought from wooden towers and fired large-calibre harquebuses from the protection of wooden palisades and bamboo bundles that had the capacity to absorb gunfire.[12]

Much alarmed by the battle taking place on his own doorstep (Ishiyama Honganji lay just across the river from Tenmagamori), Kennyo Kōsa sent out a message urging all sympathetic *monto* to rise up and oppose Nobunaga directly. Nobunaga, he said, was 'our enemy', and there was a desperate need 'to protect the light of the teachings of our founder Shinran and be loyal without regard for our own lives'. He added that any *monto* who did not cooperate would be excommunicated.[13]

The first shots of what would become known to history as the Ishiyama War were fired in the middle of the night of 12/13 October 1570, when the temple bells rang out and Kennyo commenced hostilities against Nobunaga by discharging guns at his outlying positions. It was noted that Nobunaga was taken completely by surprise. On 14 October, Kennyo's troops sortied out from Ishiyama Honganji towards Tenmagamori and attacked Nobunaga's defences, but, according to a story that does not appear in *Shinchō-Kō ki*, the garrison also took advantage of a bold move by the Miyoshi. Guns were apparently not the only weapons in their armoury, because, according to *Mikawa Gofudo ki*, Nobunaga's enemies spotted a sudden change in the weather:

---

12   SKK 1965, pp.109–10.
13   Katsura, 'Ishiyama Honganji Kassen', p.97.

However, on the thirteenth day a very strong westerly wind blew and the water in the swollen Yodo River grew turbulent. Miyoshi cut through and broke down the embankment, which allowed the river to flow suddenly into the Oda camp, causing great problems. On the twentieth day, the priests and laymen of the Honganji force advanced desperately. Seeing their opportunity, the Miyoshi force also sallied out from the castle and charged forward, trying to cut down the Oda forces in one go. The Oda army were broken into and severely defeated by the Honganji's priests.[14]

*Shinchō-Kō ki* misses this event out completely. Instead, in much more heroic vein, Nobunaga is said to have responded immediately to the attack, and the armies met across the embankment, where many heads rolled and Maeda Toshiie is 'mentioned in despatches' for his bravery. 'The *ikki* had risen up', says *Shinchō-Kō ki*, dismissively, 'but that presented no special problem'.[15] That was how much Nobunaga despised the *monto*, whether they were victorious against him or not.

In spite of *Shinchō-Kō ki*'s triumphalism, some form of setback at Noda–Fukushima, or at the very least an incomplete victory, is implied by what

Nobunaga's younger brother Oda Nobuharu (1544–1570) was killed at Sakamoto when the Oda and Asakura-Azai armies clashed there below Mount Hiei. In this illustration, Nobuharu takes a few enemies with him as he is brought down from his horse. (ESSK 1803)

14  KMGF 1976, vol. 1, p.384.
15  SKK 1965, p.110.

happened next, because, while Nobunaga was still engaged in Osaka, the revitalised Asakura and Azai were marching confidently onwards into Oda territory to threaten Kyoto itself. Their allied armies proceeded through Ōmi round the northern shore of Lake Biwa and first made contact with Oda troops on 20 October at Sakamoto, which lies on the side of the lake below Mount Hiei. Nobunaga's younger brother Oda Nobuharu (1544–1570) was killed there along with Mori Yoshinari (1523–1570), who lifted the dying Nobuharu on to his shoulders before being killed himself. The following day, the vanguard of Asakura's army entered the villages of Yamashina and Daigoji just to the east of Kyoto. The capital now lay only a stepping stone away over the Higashiyama hills, but they did not risk going any farther at that stage, thus giving Nobunaga just enough time to respond. He had been informed immediately of the developments and hurried back from the Osaka area on 23 October to set up a position at the temple of Miidera to frustrate his enemies' hesitant advance on Kyoto.

The Asakura–Azai response then became an even more defensive one, because, instead of attacking Nobunaga and then driving on to Kyoto, they moved up the slopes of Mount Hiei from Sakamoto and set up fortified lines that turned the holy mountain into an armed camp. *Shinchō-Kō ki* claims that they fled like a defeated army, which is hardly likely, but the move still suggests a lack of nerve. Nobunaga made contact with the chief priests of the Enryakuji, the temple complex and great seat of learning that sprawled across the upper reaches of Mount Hiei, and promised rewards if its warrior monks would assist him in expelling the occupying armies. Alternatively, they might decide to remain neutral, but if neither of the above courses of action was chosen – and Nobunaga put the choice quite starkly – he would burn the whole place down.[16]

No response came from the Enryakuji monks. Concluding that they were actively aiding his enemies, Nobunaga began a siege of the Asakura–Azai positions on Mount Hiei, which included raids on the temples, and this operation was still in place by the onset of winter. Meanwhile, the Ikkō Ikki of Ōmi also joined in the fray to help the Rokkaku against Nobunaga in a diversionary move. To do this, they tried to cut off the routes towards Owari and Mino, 'but they were farmers and therefore of no account', says *Shinchō-Kō ki*. Hideyoshi and others among Nobunaga's generals dealt with the threat by massacring them in their villages, and the diversionary operation ceased.[17]

Fearful of the effect all this was having on life for the citizens in Kyoto, both shogun Yoshiaki and Emperor Ōgimachi urged mediation, and, after complex negotiations, both sides agreed to withdraw. On 9 January 1571, Nobunaga began to remove his army to Gifu, and, the following day, the Asakura and Azai evacuated Mount Hiei. For the latter, the whole exercise looked like an incredible waste of effort because they had been within

---

16   SKK 1965, pp.112–13.
17   SKK 1965, p.114.

striking distance of Kyoto. Yet the agreement reached with the Asakura and Azai gave Nobunaga little rest from the wider attentions of the anti-Nobunaga coalition, so he removed one of its number by concluding a very welcome truce with Rokkaku Jōtei. On 27 January 1571, Nobunaga ordered Hideyoshi to cut off all supply routes between Echizen and Osaka and thus break another physical link in the anti-Nobunaga alliance, but very soon his attentions were drawn to a threat much nearer home, in fact, on the border of Owari province itself.

## The First Battle of Nagashima

Apart from Ishiyama Honganji itself, the Ikkō group that caused Nobunaga the greatest problems as the war began were the *monto* situated within the river delta of Nagashima. The name 'Nagashima' is believed to derive from the expression '*nana shima*' (seven islands) that occupied the delta along with a host of smaller islets. They lay within Ise at the border with Owari to the southeast of the present-day city of Nagoya, where three rivers entered Ise Bay to produce islands, reed plains and swamps. The number and the direction of flow of the rivers through the delta and the arrangement of the islands has constantly shifted throughout history owing to the effects of typhoons and floods, but even today the long, flat island of Nagashima, still set among broad rivers and waving reeds, can easily conjure up the forbidding appearance it must have presented in 1570. The settlements on the islands were known as *wajū*: flatlands protected from the waters by dykes and levees. There were several small forts and two key strongpoints in Nagashima's defences: Nagashima castle and the temple of Ganshōji, which served as Ishiyama Honganji's delegated command centre. Nagashima castle had been built in 1555 by Itō Shigeharu, who lost it to the Ikkō Ikki when he was swept from power in a manner that was becoming only too familiar to daimyo who had that particular variety of rival on their doorstep. Ōta Gyūichi describes the terrain of Nagashima as being 'more than difficult; in fact it was impregnable', and, as a result, 'renegades and outlaws' had flocked there to find a safe haven, where they became (in Gyūichi's well-considered opinion) only nominal adherents of the Honganji because they preferred worldly matters to religious observance.[18] There was some truth in his claim, because records show that, even though the entire population of the delta stood united against Nobunaga, only about one third of the *ikki* were Honganji *monto*.[19]

Three campaigns between 1571 and 1574 were required to crush Nagashima, resulting in the loss of four close members of Nobunaga's own family along with countless thousands of the 'vermin' who had dared

---

18    SKK 1965, p.159.
19    Enya Kikumi, *Ishiyama kassen wo yomi naosu* (Tokyo: Hōzōkan, 2021), p.252.

# ODA NOBUNAGA: SAMURAI COMMANDER 1534–82

The rebuilt and relocated temple of Ganshōji at Nagashima still bears the image of a fortified temple, particularly when the surrounding rice fields are flooded.

oppose him from their riverine fastness. The first victim from Nobunaga's immediate relatives was his younger brother Oda Nobuoki, who had built a castle at Kokie on the Owari side of the estuary. In their initial action, the local *ikki* took advantage of the distraction provided by the Asakura–Azai campaign and attacked out of the delta against Kokie in a daring act of outrage. The humiliated Nobuoki was forced to commit suicide by disembowelment on 18 December 1570 while his elder brother was still preoccupied with the siege of Mount Hiei.[20]

The fall of Kokie provided the dramatic start to a long campaign. Taking advantage of the temporary peace agreement with the Asakura and Azai, Nobunaga spent a few months reorganising his forces at Gifu and then responded to the loss of his brother by launching the first operation against the Nagashima *ikki* on 4 June 1571. He appointed as commanders his trusted generals Sakuma Nobumori, Ujiie Naomoto and Shibata Katsuie. The Nagashima defenders, relying on the reports they had heard of Nobunaga's first actions against Ishiyama Honganji, made suitable preparations by strengthening their outposts and setting up various other defensive measures.

Nobunaga's overconfident army made camp on 8 June at Tsushima, to the northeast of Nagashima, which was divided from the main *wajū* complex by a particularly shallow, yet broad, river, from where further attacks could afterwards be launched directly against the inner forts. Nobunaga's mounted samurai began to ford the river, only to find that its bottom was a deep layer of mud. The horses' legs quickly became mired, and, as the animals struggled, many threw off their heavily armoured riders, who were met by a hail of arrows and bullets from the *monto* and suffered severe casualties. As the survivors dragged themselves to the nearest dry land, they encountered simple defensive entanglements made from ropes stretched between stakes, which further hindered their progress towards safety. All that Nobunaga's army could do now was to set fire to a few buildings and then withdraw to the shoreline, which was covered by tall, dense reeds. The reed beds acted as a magnet to the desperate and demoralised samurai seeking cover, but, as they crawled into the undergrowth, they discovered more gunners and archers.

---

20  SKK 1965, p.159.

The most serious damage was inflicted upon the unit of Nobunaga's army that withdrew via the *wajū* of Ōtaguchi, where they were forced to move in single file because of the narrowness of the dykes and thus presented an easy target. Ujiie Naomoto was killed during this operation, and there were numerous casualties among his men, including his retainer Yuge Shurisuke, who was forced to commit suicide after fighting bravely against the *monto*. Shibata Katsuie, too, was severely wounded, and no impression was made on the defences. Thus ended Nobunaga's first attack on Nagashima in the form of an unqualified disaster. As the Oda army withdrew, they burned several villages on the outskirts of the delta, which probably had no effect other than to incline the sympathies of the local population more towards the cause of their neighbours.

## The Destruction of Mount Hiei

Later in 1571, Nobunaga conducted the most notorious operation of his entire career in an unnecessary operation where revenge was a dish served cold. Having patched up the peace settlement with the Asakura and Azai and then being preoccupied with Nagashima, it would be a full year before he turned his attentions towards the temple complex on Mount Hiei that had sheltered his enemies. In spite of its much reduced threat, Nobunaga decided to burn down the entire monastery as a punishment and as a warning to others. The assault began on 29 September 1571, and an outline of the horror will suffice. Nobunaga first burned Sakamoto, but most of the townspeople had taken refuge on the mountain. He then took particular care to destroy the 20 shrines of the *kami* Sannō the Mountain King, after which his men were deployed in a vast ring around the mountain and began to move steadily upwards at the sound of conch trumpets, burning and shooting all who stood in their way: men, women and children. By nightfall, the main temple of Enryakuji had gone up in flames, and many monks who were unable to resist had leapt into the fire. The renowned warrior monks of Mount Hiei, who had caused devastation in Kyoto only 30 years earlier, were clearly no match for Nobunaga's troops. Yet even then, Nobunaga was not satisfied, because, the next day, he sent his gunners out on a hunt for any who had escaped. The final casualty list was many thousand people and was the end of the long history of the warrior monks of the Tendai sect temples of Mount Hiei. In time, other monks returned to the mountain, but never again would they take on the role of priest armies, and the shock waves from the massacre would endure for years.[21]

Why did Nobunaga perform such an appalling act? His strategic need to punish Mount Hiei is in some ways quite easy to understand because it had provided aid and comfort to his enemies. He had said that, if they helped

---

21   SKK 1965, pp.120–22.

## ODA NOBUNAGA: SAMURAI COMMANDER 1534–82

Oda Nobunaga's army attack the monastery of Enryakuji on Mount Hiei. The warrior monks fight back as their temple blazes behind them. (KMGF 1886)

his foes, he would burn the temple down, and, when they disobeyed him, he did just as he had threatened. The mountain had, however, been acting according to an ancient precedent of religious neutrality and inviolability that had been respected for centuries. The monks traditionally gave sanctuary to anyone without any consideration for outside circumstances, and their independence was backed by the economic and military strength that allowed them to ward off intervention from those in power. Unlike other rulers who had accepted this point, Oda Nobunaga did not like the idea that independent temples and shrines could provide asylum for his enemies, but to conduct a totally unnecessary massacre after the place had been destroyed reveals for the first time in his career the deep savagery lurking in Nobunaga's psyche. Worse still, the Mount Hiei slaughter would also be a foretaste of what was to befall other communities in the next few years, and it makes one step back from any admiration for Nobunaga as a great general or even as a great man. At Mount Hiei, Nobunaga gave a warning to anyone who might be listening that he regarded a massacre as a legitimate weapon of war.

# 6

# Nobunaga Triumphant

Nobunaga may have made a powerful gesture on Mount Hiei, but the massacre had not proved him to be all powerful, and, as the Second Year of Genki (1571) came to an end, the armed entities that made up the anti-Nobunaga coalition remained unintimidated. Among them were the defiant Azai and Asakura, who had fully recovered from their defeat at Anegawa and the stand-off at Sakamoto and were ready to go to war again. The Honganji, too, had held Nobunaga off at Nagashima and were further emboldened by the outrageous operation on Mount Hiei where Nobunaga had utterly confirmed himself as the enemy of the Buddhist Law. Shogun Ashikaga Yoshiaki was also beginning to challenge him openly, and, off to the east, the first rumblings were heard from a powerful daimyo whose name has only been mentioned once so far: Takeda Shingen of Kai.

Takeda Shingen, who inflicted a serious defeat upon Nobunaga's disobedient ally Tokugawa Ieyasu at the battle of Mikatagahara in 1573. This is a votive *ema* in the temple of Tenkyūji at Kawanakajima.

## The Battle of Mikatagahara

Like the Hōjō, Takeda Shingen (1521–1573) was one of the warlords whose sphere of influence had not yet interfered with that of Nobunaga. For much of the 1550s and 1560s, he had been in arms against Uesugi Kenshin of Echigo, against whom he fought the famous five battles of Kawanakajima. The situation began to change when Imagawa Yoshimoto suffered the disaster of Okehazama at Nobunaga's hands. His province of Suruga was now up for grabs, and the Imagawa vassals and allies started to desert Yoshimoto's heir. Takeda Shingen was the first to appreciate the opportunity provided by the demoralised province and planned to annex Suruga for himself with an invasion in 1568. He withdrew from that encounter but returned in 1570 and took over Suruga in an action that established Shingen as a force to be reckoned with outside his traditional campaigning ground of the 'Japan Alps'. In 1571, Hōjō Ujimasa concluded a peace agreement with him, thus allowing Shingen to mount further major challenges in the west without the fear of a rear attack.

While all this was happening, Oda Nobunaga had been fighting the Asakura–Azai alliance once again, and his renewed aggression began with a raid on Ōmi. Taking his son Nobutada with him on his first military campaign, Nobunaga ravaged northern Ōmi in the same manner by which he had intimidated the Imagawa during the later 1550s. Seeking to maintain a presence there, he fortified Toragoze, which lay only two kilometres from Odani castle. The Azai summoned the Asakura to their resistance, and soon Nobunaga was facing their joint armies once again in an armed stand-off.

A quick resolution of Nobunaga's local difficulties was soon frustrated by an abrupt challenge from farther away when Takeda Shingen inflicted a major defeat upon him at the battle of Mikatagahara, although Nobunaga was not present on the battlefield. Had he been there, the outcome may have been different. Shingen's determined advance out of his home provinces probably had the capital as its ultimate objective, although there is no evidence that Shingen planned to go all the way during 1572. Nevertheless, any gains made along the Tōkaidō would greatly facilitate such a scheme when it was made. The Takeda's seizure of Suruga meant that Nobunaga's ally Tokugawa Ieyasu (who had left his son Nobuyasu in charge of Okazaki castle in Mikawa) was now his immediate neighbour to the west in Hamamatsu castle in the province of Tōtōmi. The Tōkaidō ran through Suruga into Tōtōmi, an area that both the Takeda and the Tokugawa had fortified heavily, particularly in the environs of the provincial borders. That made an advance by the Takeda along the coast an unwise strategy, so Shingen decided to attack out of the mountains, and the Takeda main body headed straight for Tōtōmi province down the general line of the Tenryūgawa. On 15 November, they crossed the border between Shinano and Tōtōmi. The first Tokugawa outpost to fall was the castle of Takane, after which the Takeda forces occupied Inui castle. Here, the Takeda main body divided in two to approach Futamata castle, Ieyasu's most important possession along the Tenryūgawa and the nearest major fortress to Hamamatsu. Futamata fell when Shingen's generals floated huge logs down the river to smash the supports of the castle's water tower.

In one of his earliest acts of delegation on a large scale, Oda Nobunaga sent reinforcements to aid his ally in Hamamatsu as soon as he heard about the attack on Futamata. Their leaders are named in *Shinchō-Kō ki* as Sakuma Nobumori, Hirate Hirohide and Mizuno Shimotsuke-no-Kami.[1] Nobunaga could not have known his enemy's precise objectives, but

---

1   SKK 1965, p.129.

# NOBUNAGA TRIUMPHANT

Shingen certainly appeared to be cutting a swathe through Tōtōmi and Mikawa to coincide with another probe he was making from a different direction into Nobunaga's own territory of Mino. Nobunaga's strategy was therefore to monitor the Takeda's progress until they could be safely challenged on ground of his own choosing, and Tokugawa Ieyasu provided the key to the operation. It would appear, however, that Nobunaga the strategist did not entirely trust Ieyasu the tactician, because he sent orders for him to stay securely within Hamamatsu castle and await the command from Nobunaga to move out and attack Takeda Shingen's rear when the time was right.

It was at that point that Ieyasu decided to disobey Nobunaga and fight Shingen on the plain of Mikatagahara just to the north of Hamamatsu. It was an incredibly risky move, because the insubordinate and headstrong Ieyasu was heavily outnumbered by about three to one in a total army of 11,000, of which 8,000 were his own troops and 3,000 were the reinforcements from Nobunaga. The men sent by Nobunaga were placed on Ieyasu's right wing with Sakai Tadatsugu of the Tokugawa force holding the extreme right flank beyond them, and it was in this area that the first allied casualties occurred with the death of Hirate Hirohide from Nobunaga's force. Details of the hand-to-hand fighting appear in both *Shinchō-Kō ki* and *Mikawa Gofudo ki*. The latter describes the action from the point of view of Tokugawa Ieyasu and paints him as a hero, although most of the descriptions are concerned with the overall movements of the armies rather than any fine details. This is not surprising, because snow started falling as the battle began and the situation must have been very confusing. The fighting continued until it grew dark, by which time the Tokugawa were in full retreat.

Somehow, Ieyasu made it back to Hamamatsu, which Shingen could probably have captured, but he held back from attacking. The chronicles put this down to demonstrations of bravery on Ieyasu's part (he is supposed to have left the gates wide open to fool Shingen into suspecting a trick), and his men certainly did raid Shingen's camp during the night, so, on the following morning (26 January 1573), Takeda Shingen held a brief head-viewing ceremony before moving off. The winter was now too far advanced for him to risk a long siege, so the opportunity was lost.

The head of Hirate Hirohide was sent to Nobunaga to show Shingen's disapproval of the latter's support for Ieyasu and to warn Nobunaga that,

Tokugawa Ieyasu is given a very heroic image in this print. The battle of Mikatagahara was one of the few occasions on which he let down his key ally Oda Nobunaga.

having defeated his ally, Shingen would soon be on the move again against him. At this point, however, Asakura Yoshikage – a key player in the alliance – let Shingen down. Yoshikage had been with the Azai in Ōmi for four months, helpfully tying up Nobunaga while Shingen won his victory at Mikatagahara, but, in the middle of winter, he withdrew his armies to Ichijōdani. An angry Shingen wrote to Yoshikage to complain that the anti-Nobunaga coalition was once again failing to act in a coordinated manner, leaving Shingen unsupported. He had read the situation accurately, because things soon started moving in Nobunaga's favour, and the development began with the coming of spring when Takeda Shingen headed for Mikawa and besieged the castle of Noda. Its commander held out for a month until a lack of provisions made an honourable surrender likely. According to a lively legend, the garrison decided to have a farewell drinking party, which attracted the attention of the besiegers. A vigilant sharpshooter on its walls spotted Shingen, who had been drawn to the immediate area of the castle by the sound of a flute being played. On 13 May 1573, a bullet put paid to Nobunaga's greatest rival in the east, and so tragic was his death for the Takeda that the loss was kept secret for as long as possible.

Throughout the time of the Mikatagahara campaign, Nobunaga had made great efforts to hold the Ikkō Ikki in check. He did this with a mixture of threats and promises, working on the enmity that could arise between the various branches of the True Pure Land. He also tried to control communications between their adherents in Ōmi and Echizen and between both places and Osaka. That even extended to individual monks travelling peacefully, and, early in June 1572, a *hijiri* (priestly envoy) passing between Asakura Yoshikage and Miyoshi Yoshitsugu was captured by Nobunaga's troops and put to death. This unprecedented act was taken as further proof of Nobunaga's antipathy to Buddhism itself.[2]

## The Fall of the Shogunate

By about the time of Shingen's death in 1573, an irrevocable split had developed between the independent-minded shogun Yoshiaki and Oda Nobunaga, the man to whom he owed his position. Mindful of the importance of communications between Kyoto and Ōmi should matters deteriorate further, Yoshiaki established a castle beside the strategic neck of Lake Biwa. Records relate that the fort was only half finished when Nobunaga attacked it and the defenders ran away, pleading for mercy. After more fighting with Nobunaga and the burning of part of Kyoto in retaliation, Yoshiaki took refuge in a castle called Makinoshima in Yamashiro province.[3] He left a garrison behind in Nijō castle, his stronghold

---

2   McMullin, *Buddhism*, p.110.
3   Okuno Takahiro, *Ashikaga Yoshiaki* (Tokyo: Yoshikawa Kōbunkan, 1960), pp.213–14.

within the city of Kyoto. Nobunaga wanted to respond but knew that his advance might once again be hindered by the newly hostile Rokkaku, so, to outflank them, Nobunaga decided to attack Kyoto by sailing along Lake Biwa instead of marching through Ōmi. He set up a base at Sawayama and ordered the construction of three large ships that could transport his troops across the lake. In late summer 1573, Nobunaga disembarked at Sakamoto and advanced quickly against Nijō castle, which soon surrendered. Having consolidated his position in the capital, Nobunaga attacked Makinoshima. There, Ashikaga Yoshiaki made his last stand, but, after only one day of fighting, he prudently surrendered, and the two-and-a-half-century-long Ashikaga Shogunate came to an ignominious end.[4]

Nobunaga then turned his attentions towards a final showdown with the Asakura and the Azai. He was greatly encouraged by the fact that Asakura Yoshikage had behaved with uncertainty and not a little trepidation while he watched the hounding of Yoshiaki. Yoshikage had first moved his army to Tsuruga, from where he would be best able to meet an invasion by Nobunaga moving up from Kyoto. Nobunaga was at that time preoccupied with Yoshiaki, so the cautious Yoshikage pulled his forces back once again. He then advanced into Ōmi to support the Azai, but, on 4 September, one of the key Azai generals defected to Nobunaga. The latter saw his chance, and, on 6 September, he set up lines to the north of Odani to sever its communications with Echizen. There was no fighting for two days until a fortuitous storm brought back memories of Okehazama, and Nobunaga's men overran an Asakura forward position, but, instead of taking their heads, Nobunaga let the defeated men flee to Yoshikage and frighten him into a withdrawal. The ploy worked perfectly, and the Asakura began to retreat hastily into Echizen, although even more of them defected to the Oda side. Nobunaga's army pursued the fleeing Asakura along the 40-kilometre distance to Tsuruga, killing all whom they apprehended and taking 3,000 heads.

As the pursuit continued into Echizen itself, Asakura Yoshikage abandoned his

Ashikaga Yoshiaki, whose reign as shogun came to an end in 1573. (EIG 1881)

---

4   Okuno Takahiro, *Ashikaga Yoshiaki*, pp.216–17.

# ODA NOBUNAGA: SAMURAI COMMANDER 1534–82

elegant capital of Ichijōdani. Nobunaga burned it to the ground, the fires consuming every temple and priest's residence as people and animals fled the flames.[5] He then sent out his troops to apprehend fugitives, who were brought to his camp and executed in cold blood while they were still tied up in ropes. It was a sight 'too horrible to witness', writes Gyūichi, who may have been present.[6] Many hundreds of people must have died, and there are records of traumatised refugee communities from Ichijōdani still living nearby many years later. Asakura Yoshikage himself sought safety at a succession of temples until 16 September, when he committed suicide, an act Ōta Gyūichi records with some relish, although Yoshikage appears to have been forced to perform *seppuku* against his will.[7] Azai Nagamasa followed him in death at Odani not much later when Hideyoshi captured his castle, and, together with Nagamasa's father, their skulls would become the centrepiece of Nobunaga's notorious New Year celebration of a good job done.

The suicide of Asakura Yoshikage in 1573. Yoshikage abandoned his elegant capital of Ichijōdani in the face of the Oda advance, and Nobunaga burned it to the ground. (EIG 1881, detail)

Only one reversal marred Nobunaga's year of triumph. The defenders of Nagashima may have been horrified by the attack on Mount Hiei, but they were neither discouraged nor intimidated. Takigawa Kazumasu (1525–1586) had usefully taken nearby Yata castle (present-day Kuwana), but, when Nobunaga was returning on 19 November 1573 from a successful campaign against northern Ise, the Nagashima *ikki* ambushed him. Unfortunately for Nobunaga, as soon as his men were ready to fire, a fierce downpour occurred, and the rain soaked the matches and the pans, rendering his harquebuses unusable. The Nagashima *ikki* took it as a sign from heaven of divine favour, and launched an immediate counterattack:

Seeing that Nobunaga was pulling back, the rabble of the delta pursued him with their bows and harquebuses, scurrying from one hill to another. They took up a blocking position at a narrow section the road, and the skilled archers from Iga

---

5   For a full account of the history of Ichijōdani and the fascinating archaeological exploration of the site, see Morgan Pitelka, *Reading Medieval Ruins: Urban Life and Destruction in Sixteenth-Century Japan* (Cambridge: Cambridge University Press, 2022).
6   SKK 1965, p.148.
7   SKK 1965, pp.148–49.

and Kōka hurried forward and let loose a hail of arrows that felled countless men. Because of the heavy rain, the firearms on both sides were useless.[8]

Nobunaga's army began to fall back. The brave samurai Keya Shichirōzaemon made repeated charges against the enemy to allow Nobunaga to regroup and eventually reach the safety of Ōgaki castle, so, for the second time in two years, the Oda army withdrew in a sorry state from Nagashima, and its *monto* gave thanks for another liberation from their arch tormentor.

---

8   SKK 1965, p.151.

# 7

# From Nagashima to Nagashino

The Second Year of Tenshō had begun with Nobunaga's triumphant pantomime of the gilded skulls, but, in spite of the successful removal from the scene of the Asakura and Azai together with the fortuitous passing of Takeda Shingen, Nobunaga still had much to contend with. Kennyo Kōsa of the Honganji remained unbowed even though he had been forced to look elsewhere for allies, so, from that time on, the centre of gravity of the anti-Nobunaga coalition shifted towards the west. Nobunaga now had a new opponent in the person of Mōri Terumoto (1552–1625) of Aki province, who dominated the Inland Sea and the approaches to Ishiyama Honganji. With his support, Ishiyama Honganji could look forward to having its seaborne communications maintained.

## The Destruction of Nagashima

Over the following two years, a number of important armed encounters would add to Nobunaga's reputation in very different ways. Some were positive, enhancing his standing as a military commander, but others were highly negative and involved sickening repetitions of the massacres that had already disgraced his name at Mount Hiei and Ichijōdani. His first triumph of the year was, however, an entirely peaceful diplomatic masterstroke that had no direct connection with the ongoing wars but demonstrated the hold that Nobunaga had over the imperial court and the religious establishment. A very rare block of fragrant incense wood had been kept in the imperial storehouse of the Shōsō-In at Nara for over 800 years. Nobunaga haughtily demanded a piece of it, which was supplied among great ritual and pomp on 19 April 1574. Nobunaga thus became one of only three people in the whole of Japanese history who have shared the wood, thus proclaiming his status as a man equivalent in rank to the shogun.[1]

---

1   SKK 1965, p.155.

Very soon, the perfume of scented wood was to be replaced by the smell of gunpowder and the stench of burning rice fields, because, on 23 April, there was fresh trouble from the direction of Ishiyama Honganji. No military moves are recorded on their part; Kennyo may only have been renewing his periodic call to arms, but Nobunaga made a retaliatory gesture by destroying crops and setting fires in the vicinity, yet once again he refrained from making any attack on Ishiyama Honganji itself; it was just too secure. He had to be content with raiding.[2]

The operation whereby Nobunaga moved against the Nagashima *ikki* for a third and final time proved to be a very different affair. Nobunaga's conquest of Ise had been rendered incomplete by the existence of the island enclave, but success elsewhere in the province had brought to his side an unusual naval talent in the person of Kuki Yoshitaka (1542–1600), whose support would prove crucial. Like many of the Japanese sea captains of his day, he had once been a successful pirate, operating round Ise Bay and the Kii peninsula. Nobunaga recruited Kuki and his fleet to take the fight close to the Nagashima fortifications in a way that had never proved possible before. Kuki's erstwhile pirates kept up a rolling bombardment of the defences from close to shore, concentrating on the wooden watchtowers with cannonballs and fire arrows. *Shinchō-Kō ki* describes how flags were flown from a multitude of ships that followed the Kuki into action. The presence of the ships also served to cut off the garrison from supplies and from any possible relieving force and, more crucially, enabled Nobunaga's land-based troops to take most of Nagashima's outlying forts. The capture of two in particular, Nakae and Yanagashima, allowed Nobunaga to control access from the Ise side for the first time. Nobunaga's army then attacked deeply into the *wajū*, backed up by ships out in the bay, while large-bored harquebuses were brought up and fired into the forts. Gradually, the defenders were forced back, though showing enormous resistance, and retreated to what they hoped was the impregnable island complex at Nagashima's centre. Soon, they were all squeezed into a small area on which stood the temple of Ganshōji and Nagashima castle with little else in the way of territory and almost no hope of relief.

On the night of 18 August, there was an extraordinarily heavy rainstorm, under cover of which the 'rabble' who were trapped inside the fort of Ōdorii tried to escape, but most of them – men and women – were cut down. On 28 August, the garrison of Shinohase fort surrendered and offered to join Nobunaga' forces, but he refused. By the middle of October, the Nagashima *ikki* had lost half their number through such operations or by starvation and were ready to talk peace, but their overtures fell on deaf ears. Those who tried to escape at this juncture were shot down by concentrated gunfire or were killed by edged weapons and had their bodies thrown into the river, as Nobunaga resolved to destroy the islands of Nagashima as thoroughly as he had destroyed Mount Hiei. Instead of accepting a

---

2   SKK 1965, p.156.

## ODA NOBUNAGA: SAMURAI COMMANDER 1534–82

surrender, he commenced the erection of a very tall wooden palisade that physically isolated the Nagashima *ikki* from the gaze of the outside world. Approximately 20,000 people were now crammed into the inner outposts as Nobunaga began to pile a mountain of dry brushwood against the palisade and set light to the massive pyre. Burning brands jumped the small gaps of water, and soon the whole of the Nagashima complex was ablaze. Just as on Mount Hiei, no mercy was shown, but, at Nagashima, none was asked for because the flat islands provided no resistance to the fierce fires, and, on 13 October 1574, all the inhabitants of the fortress were burned to death before any could escape. Thus ended one of the most protracted and most brutal of all Nobunaga's campaigns.[3]

In 1574, Nobunaga used gunfire against members of the Nagashima *ikki* who tried to escape from the massacre that lay in wait for them. (EIG 1881)

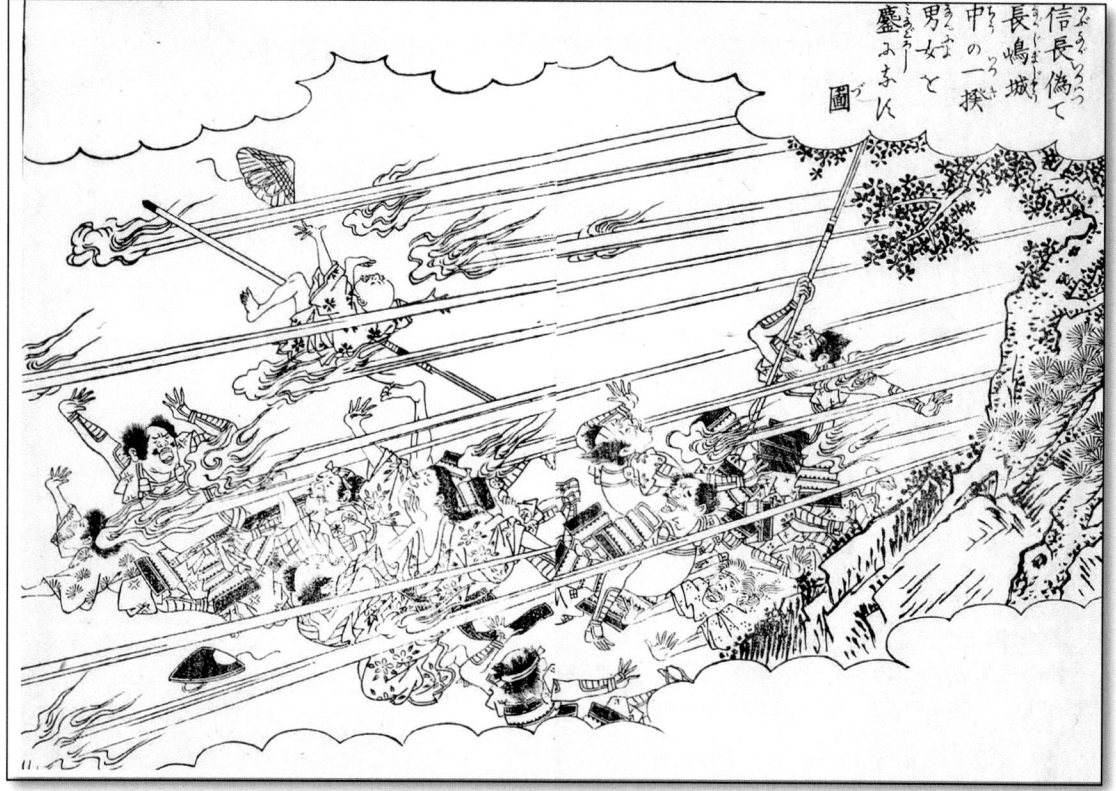

## The Battle of Nagashino

Nobunaga's next major success would be the battle in 1575 with which his name will always be associated, because Nagashino stands alongside Okehazama and Anegawa as one of Nobunaga's three great tactical triumphs on the battlefield. It was indeed a crushing victory, but so much more

---

3   SKK 1965, pp.159–63.

is claimed for Nagashino than the mere defeat of Shingen's heir, Takeda Katsuyori (1546–1582). In the popular view, Nagashino was the moment when Japan's military revolution began as thousands of harquebuses fired by Nobunaga's humble foot soldiers brought down a charge by haughty mounted samurai, thus marking the transition from medieval warfare to an early modern model. His achievement is even given an international cachet, because, by using controlled volley firing in three ranks behind simple field defences, Nobunaga found a way to defeat Japan's version of the mounted knight and thus anticipated similar developments in Europe by decades. These movements would be captured forever on the contemporary painted screen of the battle of Nagashino owned by the Tokugawa Art Museum in Nagoya. It is a highly stylised depiction because a few figures are used to represent what must have been a large-scale and highly confusing encounter, but its major theme is the conflict between troops on foot armed with harquebuses and mounted samurai, who perish in a very dramatic fashion. Groups of gunners discharge their weapons simultaneously under the watchful eyes of dismounted Oda and Tokugawa generals, while the Takeda horses are shown falling dead and throwing their riders in classic images of a broken cavalry charge.

That is the conventional image of Nagashino, which is based on an equally traditional account of the overall campaign that may be summarised as follows. Nagashino was a castle in Mikawa that was under siege from Takeda Katsuyori and in desperate need of urgent relief, for which recent events had provided awkward parallels for Nobunaga. In March of that year, Katsuyori had led an army into Mino and surrounded Akechi castle. Nobunaga had hastily dispatched a relief force, but they arrived too late, because the castle's commander had already surrendered. Later that year, Katsuyori would gain another notable victory by taking Tokugawa Ieyasu's Takatenjin castle in Tōtōmi, and once again Nobunaga sent a relief force that arrived too late, so, in the case of Nagashino, he was determined to be on time. The message requesting help for Nagashino came to Oda Nobunaga via a brave warrior named Torii Sune'emon, who slipped out of the besieged fortress. Torii would be captured and executed when he returned with the good news, but Nobunaga soon arrived and set up a defensive position on a plain called Shidarahara that lay two kilometres from Nagashino. That night, a successful raid was made on the Takeda siege lines, but, the following morning, Katsuyori placed his trust in the much vaunted Takeda cavalry to destroy Nobunaga. Charge after charge was launched against the defences, but the Takeda horsemen were shot down by rotating volleys of gunfire from supposedly 3,000 harquebuses. The widely accepted account finishes by concluding that Japanese warfare was thereby changed forever thanks to the military genius of Oda Nobunaga, who had capitalised upon years of personal success with firearms and used them in this groundbreaking manner.

The above account is a familiar storyline, but where does the traditional narrative come from? Ostensibly, it is derived from the highest authority in the land, because this is the exact version of the battle that appears in

## ODA NOBUNAGA: SAMURAI COMMANDER 1534–82

Nobunaga's son Oda Nobutada (1557–1582) at the battle of Nagashino, showing his personalised version of the Oda family heraldry. From a modern copy of the Nagashino Screen in Nakatsu castle.

the relevant volumes of *Nihon Senshi*, the official military history of Japan published from 1903 onwards by the Imperial Japanese Army's General Staff. The compilation of *Nihon Senshi* was the product of a creative approach to history typical of the Meiji Period that also saw the emergence of the idea of *bushidō* as an ancient and traditional code of warrior conduct. The attractions of this version of Nagashino to the rulers of early twentieth-century Japan are obvious, particularly when it was also claimed that Oda Nobunaga had placed his country ahead of contemporary Europe, so the narrative was not merely accepted; it was actively promoted.[4]

Yet the *Nihon Senshi* version of Nagashino did not come out of nowhere, and its ultimate origin is probably the usually reliable *Shinchō-Kō ki*, which would in turn provide the basis for more imaginative interpretations in the centuries that followed. The first variation on the story is to be found in *Shinchō ki*, a romanticised version of Nobunaga's life by Oze Hōan (1564–1640), the same author who wrote *Taikō ki* about Toyotomi Hideyoshi. Where *Shinchō-Kō ki* has Nobunaga deploying 1,000 harquebuses, *Shinchō ki* makes the number 3,000, which are fired 'all at once' and bring down '500-600 horsemen as if they were playing pieces in a game of *shōgi*'.[5] *Shinchō ki* is almost certainly the source for the account of the battle of Nagashino in *Mikawa Go Fudoki*, where the same number of 3,000 harquebuses appears.[6] It was also to be followed by the *gunkimono Oda gunki* of 1685.[7] Note, however, that none of these accounts speaks of alternate volley firing; that idea would make its first official appearance in *Nihon Senshi*, which would seem to have been influenced as much by romantic war tales as by

---

4   Suzuki, *Teppō*, pp.86–87.
5   As quoted by Suzuki, *Teppō*, p.101.
6   KMGF 1886, p.603.
7   Suzuki, *Teppō*, p.86.

serious historical source material. Suzuki suggests that the rotating volley theory was probably conceived by analogy with European practices by someone who was familiar with them. Indeed, he goes further to argue that Nobunaga did not need three-stage volley firing because it would have been wasteful of bullets against the Takeda because of how they actually operated, a point that will be discussed further below.[8] *Nihon Senshi* in turn provided the information for A. L. Sadler in his 1937 *The Maker of Modern Japan*, which was the vehicle whereby the battle of Nagashino became generally known to an English-speaking audience.[9] Since then, many writers on the subject (and I include myself in their number) have previously accepted the official version, which would be fixed for all time in the popular mind by the Nagashino scene in Kurosawa's 1980 film *Kagemusha*, where the Takeda horsemen are slaughtered in their hundreds by well-drilled infantry.

If the battle of Nagashino is to be deconstructed positively, one has to begin with the less dramatic account in *Shinchō-Kō ki*, where the observant Ōta Gyūichi sets the scene perfectly. Nobunaga chose his position at Shidarahara as soon as he arrived there. It is described as a great hollow into which Nobunaga moved his men slowly so that the Takeda would not spot them. His dispositions were defensive, indicating that he wished to engage the Takeda on ground of his own choosing rather than simply moving directly against the rear of their siege lines. Nobunaga's defences included *babō saku* (a palisade or fence for repelling cavalry), a phrase I shall examine in detail later. Ōta Gyūichi also comments on Katsuyori's dispositions. Gyūichi does of course have the benefit of hindsight, but he claims that had Katsuyori chosen not to move forward but to occupy Tobinosuyama, a hill that lay to the southeast of Nagashino castle beyond the upper reaches of the Toyokawa, then 'nothing could have been done'. Instead, of course, Katsuyori chose to fight on two fronts: in siege lines against the castle and directly against Nobunaga's relieving army. To achieve the latter, he began moving men forward, thus weakening his existing position.

Before the battle begins, *Shinchō-Kō ki* has Nobunaga welcoming Katsuyori's strategy as a gift from Heaven, and one crucial element that Nobunaga put in place to ensure a victory was a raid on the Takeda siege lines not unlike the attack Ieyasu had launched on Shingen's encampment after Mikatagahara. Two thousand of Ieyasu's men, including 'skilled archers and harquebusiers', moved forward and occupied the aforesaid Tobinosuyama that dominated the siege area. They attacked so successfully that the Takeda besiegers were driven away and Ieyasu's men entered the castle to relieve it.[10] *Shinchō-Kō ki* therefore implies that Nagashino castle was relieved before the famous battle, not after it, but, at this point, the bullets start flying, and the famous paragraphs suggesting a mass slaughter by firearms jump off the page. One example will suffice:

---

8   Suzuki, *Teppō*, pp.88, 100.
9   Sadler, *Maker*, p.103.
10  SKK 1965, p.170.

## ODA NOBUNAGA: SAMURAI COMMANDER 1534–82

Thus Tenkyū's men were also shot down and forced back until they retreated. The fifth wave was led by Baba Mino-no-Kami Nobuharu. To the beat of their war drums they came charging, but Nobunaga's men stood fast at their posts and Baba's unit were shot to pieces just like all the others had been.[11]

Identifiable by the antlers on his helmet, the celebrated Tokugawa retainer Honda Tadakatsu takes command at one of the *babō saku* (horse fences) that made up Nobunaga's defence at Nagashino. Note, however, how the famous harquebusiers are stationed outside the palisade and rely instead on a stream to keep the Takeda at bay. From a modern copy of the Nagashino Screen in Nakatsu castle.

Ōta Gyūichi then sets in stone the future understanding of what was happening at Nagashino in one short phrase. 'They kept replacing one another as they fought (i.e. they advanced in waves), but their troops kept being shot down'.[12] The impression one gets is therefore that the victory on the plain of Shidarahara was gained completely by gunfire, because Ōta Gyūichi mentions no other weapons, not even swords, and those of the Takeda who have not been shot dead die from starvation during the pursuit or drown in the rivers.[13] After this cataclysmic description, there is

---

11   SKK 1965, p.171.
12   SKK 1965, p.170.
13   SKK 1965, p.171.

very little left that needs exaggeration, so it is not surprising that the story acquired extra details and interpretation until it was understood as the classic example of a new style of warfare overcoming the old, but several aspects of *Shinchō-Kō ki*'s Nagashino narrative deserve further scrutiny.

The first point concerns the Takeda advance. Was the Takeda attack a cavalry charge in the modern understanding of the word? That is most unlikely. Even though the Takeda were famous for their use of horses and had many mounted men, they do not appear to have had a distinct cavalry arm. Those of a certain rank or status rode horses, and those without horses fought on foot, but they worked together to form a single army, as pictorial sources such as the Nagashino Screen suggest. Most importantly, this arrangement would also be found in the Oda and Tokugawa armies. Suzuki therefore argues very persuasively that, because the Takeda did not present successive lines of horsemen, there would have been no need for Nobunaga to have delivered alternate volleys; many of the bullets would have been fired into empty space![14] Nor was the terrain at Nagashino suitable for a mass charge; the front was too narrow, and there were too many obstacles, including a stream. As a final observation, one may note that at Mikatagahara in 1573 – an ideal location for a cavalry charge – the horsemen had dismounted for the initial battle and only took to their horses during the pursuit.[15]

As for the gunfire, *Shinchō-Kō ki* does not claim that rotating volley firing by three alternating ranks was performed at Nagashino. Such a process depends upon hours of drill and practice, and many of the harquebusiers Nobunaga had arranged behind the fences were not his own troops but a heterogeneous bunch who had been supplied by allies and subordinates a few days before the battle took place. There had therefore been no time to train them in anything like the counter-march technique of Renaissance Europe, and there is also no evidence that Nobunaga went to Nagashino with a fully trained harquebus corps of his own. The Nagashino Screen also shows the harquebusiers dressed in ordinary armour and helmets, not the uniform *jingasa* of Edo Period infantry, which again mitigates against there being a specialised firearms squad. Nor was Nobunaga an innovator in firearms use; only five years earlier, in 1570, Nobunaga had relied on mercenaries from Negoroji, and, as Nagashima had shown, there had been no developments since then. The only mention of concentrated harquebus fire in the 1574 Nagashima operation is when it is used to kill fleeing men, women and children. Besides, the front at Nagashino, which was constrained by hills and a river, was only about one kilometre wide, so, with 1,000 men firing in three ranks along a continuous fence (as in *Kagemusha*), each man would be three metres apart in each rank, which is hardly conducive to disciplined volleys.[16]

---

14   Suzuki, *Teppō*, p.100.
15   Suzuki, *Teppō*, pp.89–90.
16   Suzuki, *Teppō*, p.99.

Turning to the defences themselves, no continuous fence is shown on the Nagashino Screen. Instead, the harquebus troops appear to be operating from behind a cluster of defence points, each of which is represented by a loose open-work fence that provided the model for the reconstructions that now stand on the preserved battlefield. Ōta Gyūichi uses the word '*saku*' (fence or palisade) as part of the expression 'defence against horses' (*babō saku*) that Nobunaga ordered to be built 'in front of Ieyasu and Takigawa's positions', but it clearly did not stretch across the entire front. Ieyasu was in the vanguard, but Takigawa was only one of three named units behind him, so this, too, would rule out a continuous fence.[17] Yet there is another important phrase in *Shinchō-Kō ki* that has also been overlooked, because it describes the Oda side firing their guns 'with their bodies hidden' (*migakushi*), which implies the existence of stouter defence works than just an open fence.[18] This is also suggested by what would happen three years later at Takatenjin castle in 1578. Takatenjin had been captured from Tokugawa Ieyasu by the Takeda and was under siege to recapture it. According to *Kōyō Gunkan*, the commander Yokota Tadamatsu refused to ask for reinforcements from Katsuyori, reasoning that Oda Nobunaga might well respond as he had done at Nagashino, 'setting up fences, digging ditches and building embankments', an implicit acknowledgement of what probably happened at the famous battle.[19]

It is very revealing to observe that this revolutionary interpretation is now the view taken by the local Board of Education, who have installed a notice board on the Nagashino battlefield. Instead of mentioning a continuous fence, it says that Nobunaga 'constructed three-tiered *teppō kamae* [literally "gun structures"] consisting of a dry moat, a *babōsaku* and a *migakushi* [which appears here as a noun defined as an "earthen embankment"] with gun loops'.[20] Nobunaga would have had enough time to build something like this because he arrived at Shidarahara four days before the battle happened, but even simple fences would hardly have been a great military innovation. There are numerous references to quite substantial examples being set up at other engagements, including an early one in 1557 where *tatami* mats from a nearby temple were incorporated into a rough and ready *teppō kamae* because of their capacity to absorb bullets.[21]

We may therefore envisage a scenario whereby the Takeda, organised in mixed units of horsemen and infantry, attacked a series of field defences where harquebuses played a very important role, but the guns cannot have been the whole story, because *Shinchō-Kō ki* states quite clearly that the

---

17  SKK 1965, p.222.
18  SKK 1965, p.170.
19  Suzuki, *Teppō*, p.106.
20  From a personal observation.
21  Suzuki Masaya, *Sengoku teppō: Yōhei-tai tenkabito ni sakaratta Kishū Saiga shū* (Tokyo: Heibonsha, 2004), p.65.

## FROM NAGASHIMA TO NAGASHINO

battled lasted from sunrise at 8:00 a.m. to about 2:00 p.m.[22] Far from having the victory decided by firearms alone as Ōta Gyūichi so proudly proclaims, Nagashino became a huge cauldron of individual and group melees around the defensive structures and in the open ground between them. *Shinchō-Kō ki* provides little hint of this, but, if we turn to the more romantic *Mikawa Go Fudoki*, it is surprising to note that a melee is acknowledged even though that account mentions 3,000 harquebuses. There are, however, no suggestions of a continuous defensive line or rotational firing. Instead, there are some very clear examples showing how the gunfire was integrated into a long-lasting hand-to-hand situation that developed around the defensive positions as the day wore on. For example:

> The Ōkubo brothers and their followers advanced outside the fence and fired their guns at the troops of the Takeda *samurai taishō* Yamagata Saburōhei Masakage. At first, Yamagata sent out light infantry to put pressure on the enemy, but they were driven back so he tried to break through the fence with his 3,000-strong 'red regiment'. The Ōkubo brothers gave the order and drew nearer, firing over 300 guns without pause, leaving the Yamagata forces who had advanced first to be cut off.[23]

The destruction of the Takeda at Nagashino is vividly illustrated in this detail from a modern copy of the Nagashino Screen at the Matsuura Historical Museum in Hirado. Yamagata Masakage's severed head is rescued so that it will not become a trophy for Nobunaga. Meanwhile, other samurai are shot dead while the war drums continue to sound the remorseless advance.

---

22  SKK 1965, p.171.
23  KMGF 1886, p.604.

This reads much more like a conventional battle around field defences, and the following quotation provides another example of a Takeda leader approaching the defences and being killed, although his actions sound more like the results of a personal desire to die honourably rather than being killed by mass gunfire during a charge. (The reference within the quotation is to Tsuchiya's frustrated desire to follow Takeda Shingen in death in 1573):

> Tsuchiya Uemon Tadamura, who was 31 years old, pulled away from his unit and advanced to the palisade, shouting loudly, 'I am Tsuchiya Uemon, whose name has been proclaimed in Kai. Three years ago I was destined to die, but that was denied me by Kōsaka Danjō and I have survived to this day. Now I am putting my life on the line in the hands of the army. Take my head and make a name for yourself'. As he galloped up to break down the fence, he was suddenly shot by a harquebus and fell dead from his horse.[24]

That was how the battle of Nagashino ended, with heavy casualties on the Takeda side, including several named senior officers, and much killing during the limited pursuit. It was indeed a glorious victory, although Takeda Katsuyori escaped and would remain a threat to both Nobunaga and Ieyasu for another seven years before being run to ground in 1582. Once again, just as at Anegawa, Nobunaga had failed to gain a decisive victory over a serious enemy by not apprehending its leader, and that was in spite of what history commonly regards as a revolutionary moment in Japanese warfare.

In conclusion, the Nagashino narrative may have been exaggerated unrealistically to become a turning point in Japanese history, but it was a crushing victory nevertheless for which Nobunaga deserves great credit, even if it may have been won with the axe and the spade as much it was with guns. As for its myths, there was no rotational volley firing; the field defences were more than just one long fence, and the gunfire was important only during the initial encounters. So Nagashino remains a very important battle but perhaps not for the reasons that are usually claimed for it, and there remains one other crucial question about Nobunaga's undoubtedly successful generalship on the day. If Nobunaga had really been such an innovator by using guns and fences at Nagashino, what evidence is there that he learned from the experience and put the lessons to practical use on the battlefields of the future? The surprising answer to that question will be discussed in the chapter that follows.

---

24   KMGF 1886, p.605.

# FROM NAGASHIMA TO NAGASHINO

## The Conquest of the Echizen Ikkō Ikki

We will finish our account of the year 1575 with another Nobunaga victory, but it was gained under very different circumstances. After the battle of Nagashino, Nobunaga boasted that he now had only one enemy left: Ishiyama Honganji, but he had long appreciated that no siege against the Osaka temple would succeed if there were other Ikkō Ikki armies around to threaten him. Following his victory at Nagashima, the main challenge now came from Echizen province, but, as Nobunaga had captured Echizen from its ruler, Asakura Yoshikage, the existence of a new Ikkō threat requires some explanation.

In 1573, Nobunaga appointed Maeba Yoshitsugu as his governor of Echizen, but, by 1574, Yoshitsugu's treatment of his peers was giving such concern that they revolted against him. This prompted the local Ikkō Ikki to join in, and, with their help, Nobunaga's forces were driven out of the province. Here, we see the unfortunate Yoshitsugu being overcome by a group of *monto* in a very personal act of *gekokujō* ('the low overcome the high'). (ESSK 1803)

The background to the reversal in Echizen was that, when Nobunaga defeated Yoshikage in 1573, he had appointed the apparently reliable Maeba Yoshitsugu as his governor, but a dispute developed between Maeba and Tomita Nagashige, the keeper of Fuchū castle. Nagashige claimed that Yoshitsugu had failed to hand over certain administrative records. It sounds like a minor quarrel, but it was enough to prompt the local Ikkō Ikki to take advantage of the dispute. The *monto* therefore achieved what

Asakura Yoshikage had never accomplished: to drive Nobunaga's forces out of Echizen, making the area at one with its next-door neighbour Kaga: a province ruled by an *ikki*.[25]

In 1575, with his confidence bolstered by having vanquished Nagashima, Nobunaga turned his attention to subjugating the outrageous Ikkō Ikki of Echizen in a campaign that would exceed Nagashima in its cruelty and ferocity. Even so, although Nobunaga may have been ruthless, he was also a skilful politician and appealed to other Buddhist forces in Echizen to join him. He therefore stirred up the different factions within Jōdo Shinshū against each other, and the control that the Honganji had sought to impose on the others played right into Nobunaga's hands. Priests once dispatched from the Honganji had acted mainly in the interests of the head temple, rather than on behalf of the local believers and their followers, and it had been noted by the local *ikki* that those rulers were as wealthy as traditional daimyo. When Shimotsuke Raishō (1516–1575) was appointed by the Honganji, his behaviour outraged the ordinary farmers, because their rebellion against Nobunaga's appointees was supposed to have placed the province under their own control. Yet now the Honganji was behaving in as lordly a fashion as the samurai they had ousted. One prominent group within the provincial believers were the Takada branch, whose hostility to the Honganji led them to capture Shimotsuma Raishō on Nobunaga's behalf. It did not matter whether their overall ruler was Nobunaga or the Honganji: their rebellion had been set at naught.

With these 'fifth columns' already activated, Nobunaga invaded the *ikki* domain of Echizen by land and by sea on 19 September 1575. The province was easily retaken within a few days, and then the retribution began. His captains Akechi Mitsuhide and Toyotomi Hideyoshi occupied Fuchū and massacred more than 2,000 adherents of the Honganji. At this, large numbers of the populace sought to escape into the mountains, where search units sent by Nobunaga cut down men and women alike. It is recorded that more than 12,250 prisoners were sent to his camp within a five-day span and all were killed over the next few days. It is hardly surprising to read that the former magnanimity whereby Nobunaga had incorporated defeated enemies from daimyo forces into his own army was not extended to the prisoners taken from the lower-class 'rabble' of the Ikkō Ikki. Instead, words such as 'eradicate' and 'wipe out' are used in his reports of the repression.[26] Nobunaga's attendants were given the grisly task of either executing the prisoners or overseeing their removal as slaves.[27] The death toll in Echizen may well have reached 40,000, and Nobunaga described his triumph in a letter to his representative in Kyōto, Murai Nagato-no-kami:

---

25 McMullin, *Buddhism*, p.113.
26 George Elison and Bardwell L. Smith (eds), *Warlords, Artists and Commoners: Japan in the Sixteenth Century* (Honolulu: University of Hawaii Press, 1981), p.71.
27 SKK 1965, p.180.

Within the town of Fuchū dead bodies lie everywhere with no empty space between them. I wish you could see it. Today, hunting mountain by mountain, valley by valley, I have to complete the task of seeking out and exterminating them.[28]

Fearful of experiencing the same fate as the Nagashima *ikki*, the people of Echizen fled to the mountains. Nobunaga would later boast that he had slaughtered tens of thousands of these 'vermin' at the town of Fuchū alone. (ESSK 1803)

Akechi Mitsuhide and Toyotomi Hideyoshi followed up their drive through Echizen with an advance into Kaga so that, by the end of 1575, the southern half of Kaga was firmly under Nobunaga's control and its ruling confederacy was beginning to fall apart. Meanwhile, Nobunaga appointed the loyal Shibata Katsuie as governor of Echizen and issued detailed regulations concerning the behaviour to be expected from him while in office. The overall aim was to prevent an *ikki* resurgence, and, to do this, Nobunaga laid great emphasis on the principle of divide and rule, to the extent that *monto* who surrendered to him (and even some who did not) found themselves placed under the jurisdiction of a temple other than the Honganji, swearing oaths to keep them in place. Shibata Katsuie also took some radical steps of his own that anticipated moves later be associated with Hideyoshi and Ieyasu. Lowly farmers were ordered not to leave the land and take up arms,

---

28   Elison and Smith (eds), *Warlords*, p.72.

and, to make sure that they complied, Katsuie instituted the first *katana gari* ('sword hunt') in Japanese history.[29]

The famous battle of Nagashino may have been an incomplete victory, but so total was Nobunaga's triumph in Echizen that the news spread quickly to Osaka, where Kennyo proposed a truce that was agreed on 23 November 1575. The temporary pause in fighting appears to have pleased Nobunaga; he needed to rest his troops and make alliances with daimyo who would become crucial partners when he expanded his domain further, and, by the beginning of 1576, Nobunaga was ready to launch a spring offensive against his remaining enemies.

---

29   McMullin, *Buddhism*, p.119.

# 8

# Bullets and Battleships

*Shinchō-Kō ki* begins its account of the events of 1576 on a very positive note with the construction of Nobunaga's magnificent castle at Azuchi. We also have glowing descriptions of it from European visitors who marvelled at its massive stone bases and multi-storeyed keep, but warfare was not long in returning, and the first location to receive Nobunaga's attentions was Ishiyama Honganji. As noted earlier, the Osaka temple was built upon a series of islands on a river delta that opened on to the Inland Sea, which was controlled by the fleet of Nobunaga's deadly enemies from the Mōri clan, who (among other acts of defiance) had provided sanctuary for the ousted shogun Ashikaga Yoshiaki. Ishiyama Honganji depended upon being supplied with fighting men, equipment and food, and the sea lanes to Osaka were a vital conduit in that regard.

The naval campaigns that arose from this situation will be described below, but that would be only half of a two-pronged strategy because Nobunaga also appreciated that Ishiyama Honganji was well supported by fighting units in the provinces round about, so, during the fourth month of 1575, he had carried out a number of raids in the Osaka area that were aimed at cutting off the temple by land. These attacks were similar in methodology to the raids once conducted by his father into Mikawa and Mino, so we read of Oda troops burning buildings, destroying crops (there are three specific references to the practice) and establishing a number of fortified places. After this flurry of effort, Nobunaga left the Ikkō Ikki undisturbed for another year, but, in April 1576, he returned to warlike activities nearer their headquarters, and *Shinchō-Kō ki* explains his current strategic thinking as follows. The landward approach to Ishiyama Honganji was covered by three important forts. Fort Kizu lay on the coast in the Nanba area at the mouth of the estuary formed by the river of the same name, Fort Mitsudera lay nearby, and farther up the Kizugawa towards Ishiyama Honganji itself stood Fort Rōnokishi, which was the temple's nearest support castle. To cover his rear, Nobunaga ordered that the existing Oda positions, including the strategic fort of Tennōji directly to the south of Ishiyama Honganji, should have their garrisons strengthened, so Tennōji received four of his senior officers and work began on augmenting its physical defences.

# ODA NOBUNAGA: SAMURAI COMMANDER 1534-82

In 1576, Nobunaga's army attacked Fort Kizu, at which 10,000 *monto* advanced from Osaka and Rōnokishi in support of their comrades and blasted the attackers with heavy gunfire from supposedly thousands of harquebuses, leaving several senior Oda commanders dead. (ESSK 1803)

On 30 May 1576, an Oda army advanced against Kizu and Mitsudera. Mercenaries from Negoroji were in the vanguard, with Harada Bitchū-no-Kami Naomasa leading the main body of Nobunaga's 'regulars'. At this, supposedly 10,000 *monto*, including mercenaries from Saika, marched out from Rōnokishi and blasted the attackers with heavy gunfire, eager to destroy Tennōji before its rebuilding was completed, and very soon no less than five of Nobunaga's named senior officers, including Harada, were lying dead on the battlefield.[1] The victorious *ikki* then surged on towards Tennōji itself, where, according to local oral tradition, its makeshift defences included *tatami* mats and the bodies of dead horses.[2]

Nobunaga was in Kyoto when the bad news arrived but set out full of confidence to relieve the beleaguered fort, although his subsequent actions sound like a slapdash affair that had not been properly planned. Nobunaga's army was small, and he is described as wearing only a light summer kimono. He also advanced so rapidly that his foot soldiers and baggage train were unable to keep up with him, but, when reports arrived that Tennōji could only hold out for a few more days, Nobunaga went straight into the attack against the rear ranks of the besiegers in spite of being outnumbered by

---

1   SKK 1965, p.193.
2   As recorded on a local history website, Inufuku Chihuahua, 'Tennōji no tatakai', *Sengoku History* (2019), <https://sengoku-his.com/13>, accessed 8 March 2025.

## BULLETS AND BATTLESHIPS

five to one. Highly confident, he deliberately made himself very visible as he rode up and down giving orders, and one of the thousands of bullets that must have been delivered from the *ikki* harquebuses wounded him in the leg. At this, his officers pleaded with him to withdraw, but Nobunaga was having none of it. The result was Nagashino in reverse, because this time there was a victory for the side that charged the guns. Nobunaga's army managed to fight their way through the hail of fire, saved Tennōji and pursued the fleeing *monto* as far as the southern gate of Ishiyama Honganji. More forts were then established round about to lay claim to the temple's hinterland.³

The heroic death of Nobunaga's general Harada Bitchū-no-Kami Naomasa at the battle of Fort Kizu. (EIG 1888)

*Shinchō-kō ki* celebrates the battle of Tennōji without the slightest trace of irony for a victory that had been won only because Nobunaga 'did a Katsuyori' and advanced into a storm of bullets fired from the safety of field fortifications. Nor does it mention Nobunaga's very clever use of fake news after the battle for propaganda purposes, because court diaries

---

3   SKK 1965, p.193.

# ODA NOBUNAGA: SAMURAI COMMANDER 1534–82

The defence of Fort Tennōji, where Nobunaga was shot in the leg by a bullet fired probably by one of Ishiyama Honganji's mercenaries from Saika in Kii province. Nothing daunted, Nobunaga advanced again under heavy gunfire and relieved Tennōji, after which he led a pursuit as far as the gates of Ishiyama Honganji itself. (ESSK 1803, detail)

of the time refer to Nobunaga sending to Kyoto the heads of Ishiyama Honganji's leading commanders, including that of Suzuki Magoichi, the legendary leader of the Saika mercenaries from Kii. The head belonged to someone else who was far less distinguished, but it did the trick, and the people of Kyoto both high and low were suitably stunned by the proof it brought of a triumph at Tennōji.[4]

## The First Battle of Kizugawaguchi

The attack on Fort Kizu had represented an attempt by Nobunaga to control the mouth of the Kizu River from the land, but, from the time of the battle of Tennōji onwards, that same objective would also be sought by sea in Osaka Bay or, as the chronicles prefer, Kizugawaguchi ('the mouth of the Kizu River'), where two remarkable sea battles would take place in 1576 and 1578. An entirely new experience for Nobunaga was about to unfold.

The challenge to him had been launched by the powerful seaborne forces of the Inland Sea. To their followers, they were 'lords of the sea' who commanded navies; to their enemies, they were *kaizoku* (pirates). The most powerful sea lord to the west of Osaka was Mōri Terumoto, but his aim was not to force a major naval battle with Nobunaga. Instead, Terumoto applied the same strategy that he had followed for years against other enemies: that of controlling strategic sea areas and the traffic lanes through them. Peter Shapinsky, in a major study of the sea lords, refers to these places as 'choke points', of which the Kizu estuary and the narrow straits around Awaji island were important examples.[5] The Mōri were also helped by warriors from

---

4   Suzuki, *Teppō*, pp.120–21.
5   Peter D. Shapinsky, *Lords of the Sea: Pirates, Violence and Commerce in Late Medieval Japan* (Ann Arbor: University of Michigan Press, 2014), p.160.

Saika in Kii; in addition to supplying mercenaries for Ishiyama Honganji, they could send a fleet to harass shipping moving up towards Osaka off the coast.

*Shinchō-kō ki* discusses these naval developments after reporting on the engagement at Tennōji and confirms how, by 9 August, naval forces from the Inland Sea had assembled 700 or 800 ships with the intention of sailing into Osaka Bay laden with supplies for Ishiyama Honganji. Nobunaga responded by summoning his own friendly sea lords, who sent 300 ships to seal off the mouth of the Kizugawa. *Shinchō-kō ki* says that the Inland Sea fleet 'smashed into' his blockading vessels. On land, the garrisons from forts on both sides of the conflict rushed to join in the fight, so troops from Rōnokishi and Tennōji again came to grips with their enemies.

The first battle of Kizugawaguchi consisted of a fight between the rival squadrons, within both of which the main type of warship was a vessel known as the *atakebune*. Slow and clumsy, the *atakebune* would earn a bad reputation when they were attacked by the more manoeuvrable 'turtle ships' of Korea's Admiral Yi during the invasion of Korea in 1592. In Japanese waters, particularly the inlets and coves of the Inland Sea, an *atakebune* could be a formidable vessel. When there was no risk of capsizing, individual hatches in the sides of the ships could be let down to facilitate boarding parties, and sturdy gunwales protected their archers and harquebusiers. *Atakabune* therefore combined the notions of fortification and shipping into the design of a floating castle with a small keep on the open deck.⁶ The ships' armaments included grappling weapons and firearms of various sizes, but the Inland Sea fleets were also known for the use of fire arrows and exploding bombs. The latter consisted of two hemispheres fastened together and wrapped round with layers of paper glued on to the outside surface. A fuse timed by its length ran into the interior, and the bombs were attached to a rope to be flung much in the manner of a hammer-thrower. They could cause fires on rival ships, and the fragments also wounded enemy soldiers.

A simple model of an *atakebune* warship bearing the flag of the Murakami navy of the Inland Sea. These vessels formed the backbone of the fleets that tested Nobunaga's blockade of Ishiyama Honganji. (Wikimedia Commons)

*Shinchō-kō ki* contains very few details of how the two fleets engaged, but other sources analysed by Shapinsky fill in the gaps, and the results are a revelation. Instead of a sea battle in a huge melee as is commonly

---

6   Shapinsky, *Lords of the Sea*, p.178.

# ODA NOBUNAGA: SAMURAI COMMANDER 1534–82

supposed, at Kizugawaguchi, the Inland Sea fleet attacked what was in effect a floating barricade because Nobunaga had tried to build a wall of ships. Protected by lighter escort vessels, the Oda vessels had turned their rudders to take them into the mouth of the river and literally joined forces with Nobunaga's troops on land via extended bridges. The response came on 6 August 1576, but, when the battle began, the end result was by no means obvious. Nobunaga's naval allies initially proved a match for the enemy sea lords, forcing a rethink for the supply convoy. The decision was therefore made to go for the Oda ships on an individual basis, firing harquebuses and flinging the deadly bombs, which exploded on the decks and set fire to the ships' superstructures. The casualties among Nobunaga's allies were high and were made more acute by the presence on board of the land-based soldiers, who tried to make an escape to the shore. Many were cut down in the chaos of the evacuation, and the Inland Sea coalition claimed to have destroyed several hundred ships in the fight. With the blockade broken, the relieving fleet sailed up the Kizugawa with the much-needed supplies for Ishiyama Honganji.[7] The bad news was reported to Nobunaga, who realised that there was little he could do except strengthen his coastal defences.

The battle of Kizugawaguchi is at its height as Mōri's superior craft collide with Nobunaga's ships. Arrows and bullets (and bombs, which are not shown here) rain down on the decks and break Nobunaga's blockade. Hand-to-hand fighting is, however, still the key to victory. One man has his legs cut off while another loses his head as a trophy. (ESSK 1803)

---

7   Shapinsky, *Lords of the Sea*, pp.180–81.

# BULLETS AND BATTLESHIPS

## The Invasion of Saika

Nobunaga's reversal at sea at the first battle of Kizugawaguchi forced him to revise his strategy once again, so he reverted to the model that had dominated his thinking about Ishiyama Honganji since his first encounter back in 1570: to overcome their more distant supporters. This time, the plan was to attack the key element that came from Kii province, but a nasty surprise lay in wait for him. Once again, hand-held firearms were involved, because Nobunaga's new target for 1577 was Saika, the small yet belligerent district that had long supplied mercenaries in the Honganji's defence. Nobunaga believed that destroying these long-term supporters and their guns would fatally isolate the temple.[8]

Nobunaga's Saika campaign is a little-known episode in his career, and the main reason is that the operation ended in failure. The troop numbers deployed by Nobunaga were considerable – a figure of 100,000 is cited – and, even if one has to apply a reasonable divisor, the number exceeds that of Nagashino, which shows the importance Nobunaga attached to the expedition. Yet once again Kii was divided, with three of the five districts of Saika supporting Nobunaga. He also had the cooperation of the Suginobō temple within the Negoroji complex, while the other powerful Negoroji temple of Senshikibō (which had important family links to the

A rare depiction of Nobunaga's disastrous invasion of Saika in 1577, where he was stopped by concentrated gunfire across a river. (ESSK 1803)

---

8   Suzuki, *Teppō*, p.124.

hostile districts of Saika) opposed him.[9] Mindful of the danger from Mōri Terumoto, Nobunaga led his army only as far as Izumi and sent two separate contingents of 30,000 men each into Kii along the coast and through the mountains. The coastal army attacked Suzuki Magoichi's castle. *Shinchō-Kō ki* notes Nobunaga setting up bamboo bundles for protection, which must have been against gunfire.[10]

The inland column marched towards the Kozaika River under Hori Kyūtarō, and it was at this watery barrier that the Saika guns proved most effective because they had set up a wooden palisade along the far bank, which was itself a natural obstacle too steep for horses to climb. Many of Nobunaga's experienced warriors were killed, and the survivors were forced to abandon the assault.[11] Local tradition (as recorded in writing during the eighteenth century) adds that the defenders had buried old pots and jars in the riverbed, which trapped the legs of men and horses and made them easy targets. The local *kami* also came to the defenders' aid by providing an unusually high tide.[12]

There was little Nobunaga's troops could do except try to maintain their position across the river, so once again concentrated harquebus fire by lower class warriors from simple defences had triumphed against the supposed master of firearms. Had Nobunaga learned nothing at Nagashino? At Tennōji, he had advanced against gunfire and won the day, but the battle in Saika sounds like Nagashino in reverse, and Lamers states bluntly that 'This campaign was not a complete success'. He also quotes a letter from Mōri Terumoto to Uesugi Kenshin that states that Nobunaga had to withdraw because the fortifications proved too strong, although Nobunaga apparently persuaded the Saika to agree to a nominal surrender. The red seal letter that he issued has survived, and, although it is composed in a very arrogant manner, it seems to have been just a face-saving peace agreement that allowed him to withdraw with honour.[13] That Nobunaga had gained no real victory was exposed within a few months when he sent Sakuma Nobumori to attack Saika again in a campaign that *Shinchō-Kō ki* completely ignores.[14] The details are vague apart from a local tradition that there were about 200 casualties on each side, but it is not difficult to imagine that Nobunaga's army were again defeated by strong defences and the use of firearms.[15] Indeed, the Saika mercenaries were still riding high two years later, because, in 1578, Ishiyama Honganji would request them to supply

---

9 SKK 1965, p.202; Suzuki, *Teppō*, pp.124–25; CLN 2011, p.261n.
10 SKK 1965, p.202–05.
11 SKK 1965, p.203.
12 Suzuki, *Sengoku teppō*, p.149.
13 Lamers, *Japonius Tyrannus*, p.151.
14 Suzuki, *Sengoku teppō*, p.118.
15 Suzuki, *Teppō*, pp.127–28.

500 men with firearms skills, which was proof enough of their survival after two invasions by Nobunaga.[16]

# The Battle of Tedorigawa

While Nobunaga was engrossed in the Kinai, his loyal and hard-working generals had been actively pushing further into Kaga, where the final outposts of the Ikkō Ikki north of Kyoto were still holding out. That brought Nobunaga's armies close to the sphere of influence of another distant daimyo, the famous Uesugi Kenshin (1530–1578). In 1577, the Oda expeditionary force under the command of Shibata Katsuie devastated the crops in the fields and burned fortified outposts. *Shinchō-Kō ki* then tells us merely that Nobunaga's forces withdrew from Kaga on 12 November, thereby omitting any account of the military disaster that had befallen them at the hands of Uesugi Kenshin on 3 November.

Kenshin had marched into Kaga to oppose Nobunaga and had based himself and 30,000 troops at the castle of Matsutō. Shibata Katsuie had 18,000 men within a total army of about 50,000, and the armies met across the Tedorigawa, otherwise known as the Minatogawa. Kenshin anticipated that Katsuie would try to move across the river by night for a dawn attack on Matsutō. He therefore detached a small decoy force in plain sight of the Oda army and moved it up towards a fort he had built at the head of the river. This gave the impression that Kenshin had split his forces and encouraged Katsuie to make a frontal assault straight across the shallows. The result was one of the classic night battles of Japan where Kenshin's force, in three forward units with a main body in reserve, absorbed Katsuie's advance. The main body then moved in and defeated the Oda army, which Kenshin firmly believed to

Uesugi Kenshin (1530–1578), who challenged Nobunaga late in his career and defeated his army at the battle of Tedorigawa. Kenshin's mysterious death in 1578 was a great relief to Nobunaga.

---

16  Suzuki, *Sengoku teppō*, p.69.

be under the command of the great Nobunaga himself, even though he concluded that the military response to his manoeuvre was surprisingly weak for so great a commander. Shibata Katsuie managed to hold on to his two outposts, but Kenshin's victory at Tedorigawa had drawn a line across Nobunaga's northern expansion, just as Saika had to his southern borders.[17] The year 1577 had certainly been a bad one as far as Nobunaga was concerned.

## The Second Battle of Kizugawaguchi

In 1578, Nobunaga gained a welcome naval victory at the second battle of Kizugawaguchi. Like Okehazama, Anegawa and Nagashino, second Kizugawaguchi is one of the battles that has earned Nobunaga the title of military genius, so what had changed to give him a victory at the same place where he had been defeated in 1576? Just as for Nagashino, popular history gives the credit once again to Nobunaga's innovative grasp of modern military technology, and it is well recorded that, when Nobunaga decided to challenge the maritime supply routes into Ishiyama Honganji for a second time, he commissioned new ships of a larger and revolutionary design. He gave the contract to Kuki Yoshitaka, Ise province's answer to the Murakami navy who had helped to crush Nagashima, and the result was supposedly the deployment of the world's first ironclad battleships. That is an extraordinary claim to make, and in fact the only source is a diary called *Tamon-In nikki*, which simply calls Nobunaga's vessels 'iron ships'.[18] The diarist was the priest Eishun from Nara, who never saw the ships in person, and, by contrast, other references to the vessels make no reference to iron plates. *Shinchō-Kō ki*, which one would expect to laud Nobunaga's military achievements to the skies, merely states that Kuki built six great ships. Most importantly, the Jesuit missionary Father Organtino Gnecchi witnessed the fleet at sea and also made no mention of iron plates. He noted merely that 'they are the best and largest in Japan, being about the size of royal carracks', carrying 'three pieces of heavy ordnance'.[19]

The ships must indeed have been very heavy, because an official from Ishiyama Honganji observed that they did not move easily at sea.[20] That was probably because of their size and weight rather than from any extra iron, and Suzuki has argued convincingly that to add iron plating to the weight of what were already very heavy and sluggish ships would have been unnecessary. Solid wooden planking and bamboo bundles gave adequate protection against harquebus fire, and the key weapons in the first battle

---

17  SKK 1965, pp.37n, 272.
18  Suzuki, *Teppō*, p.130.
19  *Cartas* 1598, vol. 1, f. 415v.
20  Shapinsky, *Lords of the Sea*, p.182.

of Kizugawaguchi had been the bombs thrown in a parabolic arc on to the decks and towers of the ships, not against their sides. Iron plates would have provided no defence against incendiary weapons unless they had covered the decks and the superstructure.[21] Even those who believe in the iron-plate theory are forced to concede that the elusive plates would only have been used in particularly vulnerable areas of the ship such as to protect the gunners. Instead, as noted above, Father Organtino was more impressed by their cannon, which he believed were cast in Japan itself rather than having been supplied by the Portuguese through friendly intermediaries. One might therefore think of the iron ships as floating block-ships, designed not for naval fighting while moving but to enforce the solid walled blockade that had failed Nobunaga in 1576.

A little-known skirmish that took place just before the second battle of Kizugawaguchi allowed Kuki Yoshitaka the opportunity to try the ships out when he sailed round the Kii peninsula towards Osaka. As he reached a place called Tannowa on 30 July 1578, he was attacked by numerous small vessels from Saika. The Saika ships were armed only with bows and harquebuses, against which any armour plates would have come in handy, but again none are mentioned. Kuki Yoshitaka let them draw near and then 'gave them a warm welcome'. These words in *Shinchō-Kō ki* imply the sixteenth-century Japanese equivalent of a broadside. The Saika navy withdrew, and Kuki sailed on into the harbour of Sakai, where they caused amazement to many, including the perceptive Father Organtino.[22] *Shinchō-Kō ki* is, however, confusing over how long they stayed at Sakai before setting up the Osaka blockade. Apparently, Nobunaga visited Sakai after a grand progress from Kyoto (including a little falconry on the way) and personally inspected Yoshitaka's flagship. He was much impressed, and the story of how they brushed off the Saika navy would also have reassured him as to their usefulness, so Nobunaga lavished gifts upon his admirals.[23]

*Shinchō-Kō ki* tells us nothing about how Nobunaga disposed the iron ships in his new blockade of the Kizu Estuary, although subsequent events would rule out a bridge across the sea as had been tried in 1576. Instead, the narrative jumps straight to the fighting of the second battle of Kizugawaguchi, and the Honganji records indicate that the Ikkō Ikki knew what was about to hit them and what the implications were.[24] Father Organtino had already speculated that the new ships would bring about the fall of Ishiyama Honganji, and reports from the defeated Saika navy would only have confirmed the *ikki*'s worst fears. Their leaders send out urgent pleas for reinforcements to smash the blockade, 'or the temple would certainly fall'.[25]

---

21  Suzuki, *Teppō*, p.130.
22  SKK 1965, p.228.
23  SKK 1965, p.231.
24  SKK 1965, pp.234–35.
25  Shapinsky, *Lords of the Sea*, p.183.

*A model in the Saga Prefectural Nagoya Castle Museum showing a large form of atakebune that was used during the invasion of Korea in 1592. Nobunaga's so-called 'iron ships' were probably of this size and design.*

The best account of the second battle of Kizugawaguchi is to be found in *Shinchō-Kō ki*, which one might expect for a catalogue of Nobunaga's victories, although it tells us very little about the fight. Six hundred enemy vessels (most of which must have been supply ships) approached Kizu and encircled Kuki's fleet. His six great ships drew the enemy near and concentrated on their flagships. They blasted them with his big guns and drove them away up the strait.[26] This is effectively the only account that exists, and doubt has been cast on whether there was one decisive battle at all. The Kuki family accounts claim that five enemy ships were captured, which is hardly a crushing victory. The account is also very similar to that describing the battle of Tannowa, and, very surprisingly, Oze Hōan's romantic *Shinchō ki* does not mention the second battle of Kizugawaguchi at all, just the actions against the Saika navy. It is a strange omission for a heroic *gunkimono*![27]

Nevertheless, it is customary to end Nobunaga's war against the Ishiyama Honganji with this great victory whereby the revolutionary iron ships severed Mōri Terumoto's supply lines for good. In reality, Ishiyama Honganji would hold out for a further two years in spite of this supposedly decisive naval victory.[28] In fact, there is clear evidence that Mōri samurai and Saika mercenaries frequently entered and left Ishiyama Honganji, and there is also the fact that Honganji kept on requesting other followers in various provinces to secure supplies. Those requests would only have been made if there was still the likelihood of the supplies being delivered successfully, and proof that this was actually carried out can be seen from the letters of thanks that were sent to Mōri and others for their efforts in procuring and despatching the goods. There is also a third party confirmation that

---

26  SKK 1965, pp.234–35.
27  Suzuki, *Teppō*, p.132.
28  Suzuki, *Teppō*, p.133.

Ishiyama Honganji was still replete with supplies when it surrendered in 1580, because *Tamon-In nikki* laments that, when the fortress was burned, large amounts of rice, salt, *miso* and other foodstuffs that had been stored there were destroyed, which was 'a waste for the country as a whole'.[29] This shows that the outside world did not see the surrender of Ishiyama castle as being due to a shortage of food and war materials. If these facts are weighed up, the established theory that a naval blockade led to the surrender of Ishiyama castle is called into question.[30]

So the supplies got through and continued to do so, and Ishiyama Honganji was helped also by defections from a few of Nobunaga's generals, whose departure left gaps in the ring of steel that Nobunaga had created around the temple. One of the traitors was Matsunaga Hisahide (1508–1577), who then had charge of the very strategic fort of Tennōji. For some reason, he and his son abandoned the fort and shut themselves up in their own castle of Shigisan, where fierce retribution followed and Hisahide was overcome. Colourful tradition tells of Hisahide, who was a noted master of the tea ceremony, smashing a priceless tea bowl before committing suicide. His son acted as his second and dived to his death from the castle wall clutching his father's head in his hands and with his sword blade in his mouth.

An even more serious set of defections occurred in 1578 when as many as three of Nobunaga's generals appeared to waver at the same time. Takayama Ukon held Takatsuki castle; Nakagawa Kiyohide held Ibaraki, and

The spectacular end to Nobunaga's siege of Shigisan, whereby rebel Matsunaga Hisahide's son jumped off the castle tower with his father's severed head. (ETK 1799)

---

29   Suzuki, *Teppō*, p.134.
30   Suzuki, *Teppō*, pp.135–36.

# ODA NOBUNAGA: SAMURAI COMMANDER 1534–82

The rebellion of Araki Murashige was one of the most severe challenges mounted against Nobunaga towards the end of his career. Murashige's defection left a hole in the ring of steel Nobunaga was constructing around Ishiyama Honganji. (EIG 1888)

both came under suspicion, but the most important of the trio was Araki Murashige (1536–1585) of Arioka (modern Itami) castle, whose role by sea and land was crucial in the blockade. In 1578, he was away fighting at the siege of Miki castle in Harima province under the direction of Toyotomi Hideyoshi but was accused of sympathies towards the Mōri. At this, Murashige came out into the open as a traitor and retreated to Arioka in blatant defiance of Nobunaga's orders. That was a huge boost to Ishiyama Honganji because Murashige's absence from the scene at a crucial coastal choke point allowed the Mōri navy to get through with more supply vessels.[31] Nobunaga successfully put pressure on the other two rebels to abandon him. They were richly rewarded for returning to the fold, and a one-year-long siege of Arioka began. Mōri Terumoto promised to come to Murashige's aid, but help never materialised, and, after nine months of privation, Murashige sneaked out of Arioka and took refuge further out of Nobunaga's reach in the castle of Amagasaki, leaving his family and supporters to their fate. The abandoned garrison tried to persuade Murashige to surrender, which Nobunaga agreed to while keeping their families as hostages, but Araki Murashige did not surrender, and the fate of his family would be terrible, with mass executions damning his treachery. The revolt was thereby quelled, but Murashige himself escaped to the protection of the Mōri and died several years later in 1586, by which time Nobunaga was long gone.

---

31   Shapinsky, *Lords of the Sea*, p.184.

# 9

# The Final Years

The final two years of Oda Nobunaga's life are something of an anti-climax to his tempestuous military career, because all his victories are won for him by subordinates and even his significant triumphs of negotiation are conducted by third parties. Nobunaga tends to stay aloof from the fighting until victory is gained, after which he makes a grand progress to survey his conquests and acknowledge in a very genuine sense the contribution from his loyal generals. The fool of Owari has long since disappeared into history; now, we see Nobunaga the strategist and politician, and it is a formula that works very well until his final campaign: a delegated operation against the Mōri characterised by unprecedented overconfidence that places him into a situation of peril.

## The Honganji Settlement

The Araki rebellion of 1578 may have posed a serious challenge to Nobunaga's overall strategy, but, by the beginning of 1580, the destruction of Araki Murashige had revealed how little support Ishiyama Honganji had left. The supplies may have been getting through, but Mōri Terumoto had proved either unwilling or unable to relieve Arioka, let alone the great Osaka temple, and a further setback for the Mōri came when Ukita Hideie (1572–1655) of Bizen province defected to Nobunaga's side. In a letter written sometime after 1580, Kennyo stated that the defection of the Ukita clan had been a major factor in his eventual decision to surrender. More setbacks followed for the Mōri faction when Toyotomi Hideyoshi captured Miki castle early in 1580 and his fellow general Akechi Mitsuhide pacified Tanba and Tango provinces. Finally, Nobunaga was greatly helped by the sudden death of Uesugi Kenshin, a passing so fortuitous – the Uesugi clan descended into civil war between rival heirs – that grisly stories grew concerning assassination.

Ishiyama Honganji was now more alone than it had been at any time during the previous 10 years. Nobunaga had successfully isolated its allies one by one and neutralised most of them; Saika's survival was unique. In

# ODA NOBUNAGA: SAMURAI COMMANDER 1534–82

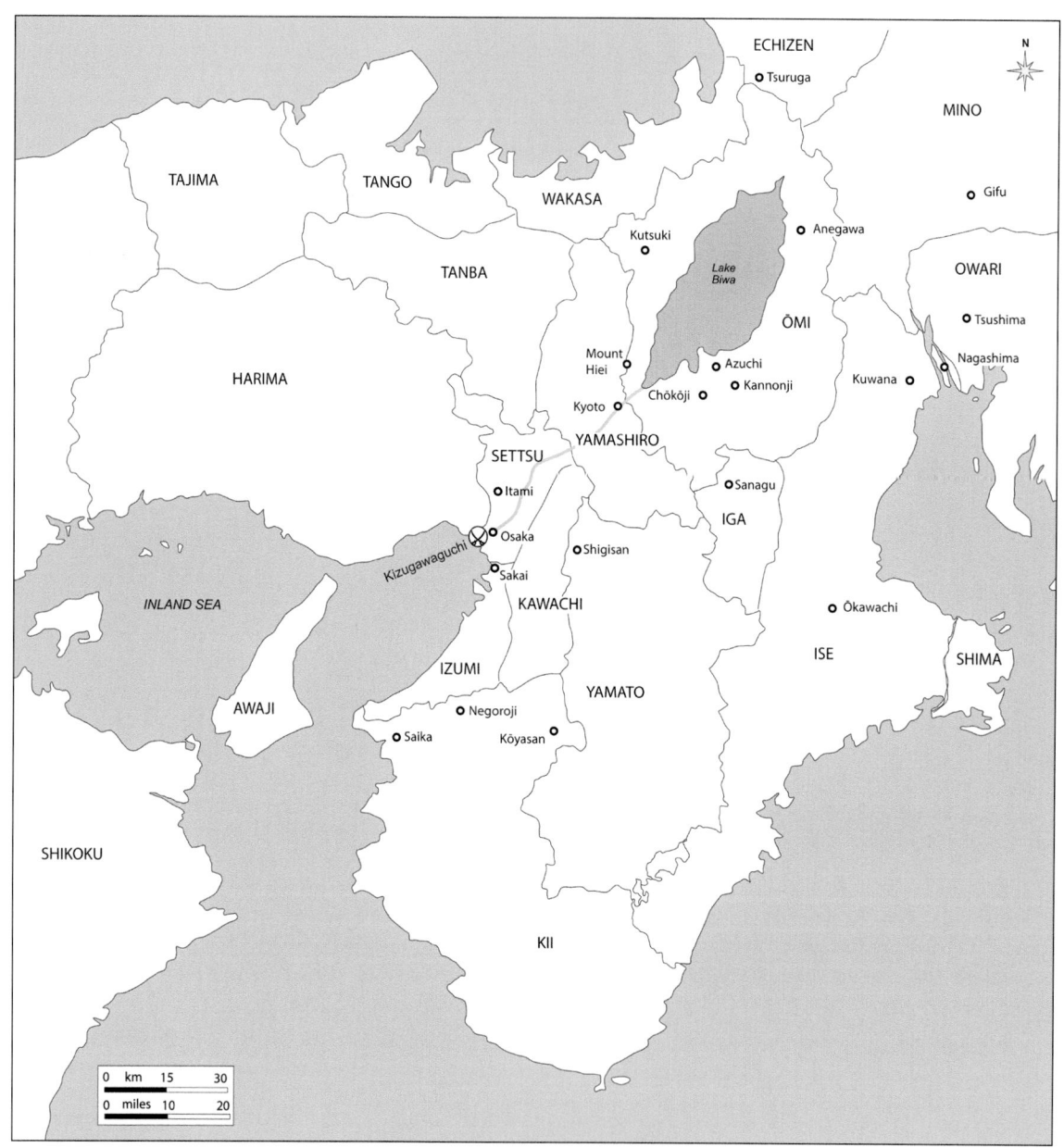

Oda Nobunaga's realm c. 1575–1582.

place of war, peace negotiations were taken up between representatives from Nobunaga and Kennyo, but the latter's defiant son Kyōnyo (1558–1614) opposed any settlement with the tyrant and thus became by default the leader of the war faction in the Honganji. Something more authoritative was needed if Ishiyama Honganji was to capitulate with its honour intact, and, in April 1580, an imperial messenger was sent with a letter from no less a person than the emperor of Japan, suggesting a peaceful surrender. The letter had of course been prompted by Oda Nobunaga.

The move succeeded, and, in accordance with the agreed terms, Kennyo left Osaka on 22 May 1580 and moved to Saginomori in Saika, where he set up a new Honganji under the protection of his erstwhile mercenaries. Back in Osaka, Kyōnyo continued to urge defiance against Nobunaga and appealed to the *monto* to rise up once again, but his father disowned him and named his younger brother Junnyo as heir instead of Kyōnyo. Utterly frustrated, Kyōnyo finally opened the gates in surrender on 10 September 1580. Fearing retribution from Nobunaga when his armies took over, the inhabitants of Ishiyama Honganji fled in terror, but, in spite of the precedents he had set on Mount Hiei and at Nagashima, Nobunaga acted with uncharacteristic generosity towards the sect that had caused him so much trouble, and many people were evacuated safely by sea to Awaji or Saika. Ishiyama Honganji itself, however, suffered total destruction, because, before Nobunaga could take possession of it, someone set fire to the place and the abandoned temple was burned to ashes. It will never be

In September 1580, Patriarch Kyōnyo finally opened the gates of his fortress cathedral. When Nobunaga took possession of it, persons unknown set fire to the place, and the abandoned Ishiyama Honganji was burned to ashes. (ESSK 1803)

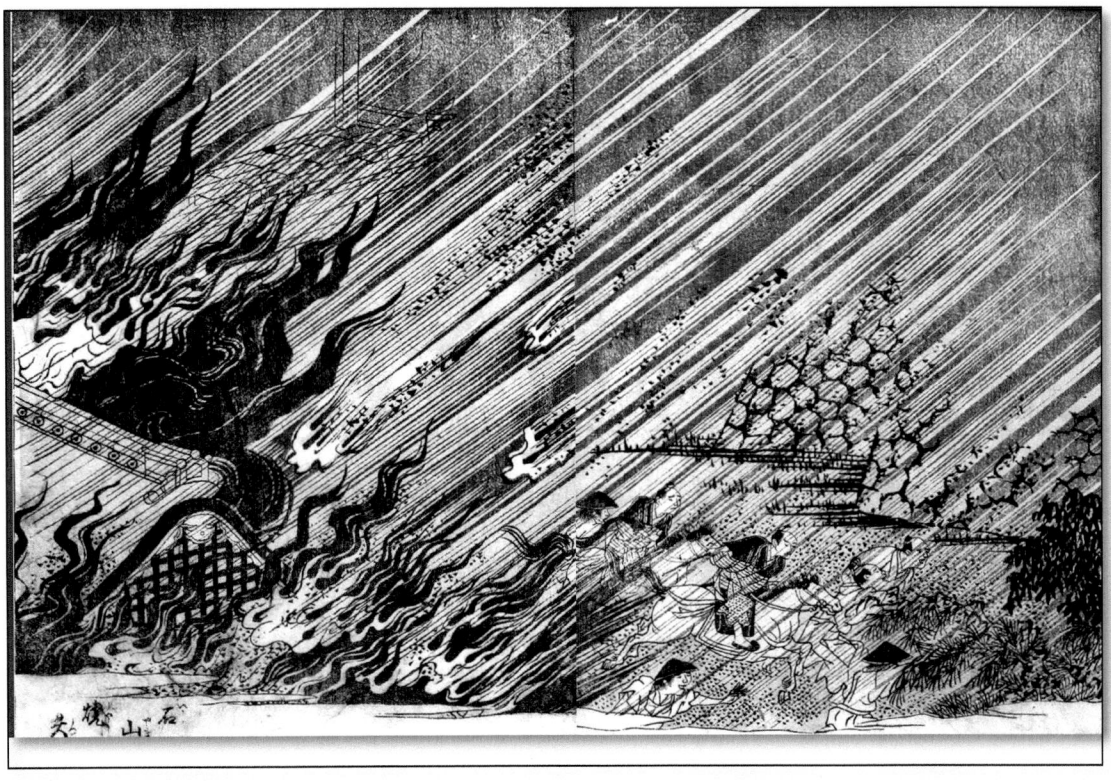

known who started the fire, whether it was Nobunaga's men or diehard Ikkō *monto* who preferred destruction to desecration.[1]

## The Harrying of the *Ikki*

Nobunaga's war against the Ikkō Ikki is commonly regarded as having finished with the surrender of Ishiyama Honganji. However, there were a few more episodes of bitter fighting left against other provincial groups of Honganji *monto* and other *ikki* whose allegiance was not faith-based, and the first action was directed against Kaga province. Die-hard elements had entrenched themselves in two sites among the foothills of the mighty Hakuzan mountains. The forts of Torigoe and Futōge would change hands three times within the following two years until these final outposts of the Kaga Ikkō Ikki were wiped out. The first attack upon Torigoe and Futōge was made by Shibata Katsuie in the third lunar month of 1581. He captured both places and set up his own garrison of 300 men, but, before the month was out, the Kaga Ikkō Ikki had recaptured them and slaughtered the Oda troops. In December 1581, Shibata Katsuie and Sakuma Morimasa returned to Kaga and crushed the resistance once again, killing all the *monto* involved. We read that the heads of the ringleaders were sent to Nobunaga's castle of Azuchi and placed on public exposure. Yet in spite of this setback, Ikkō resistance continued in Kaga, and elements of the organisation recaptured Torigoe and Futōge once again during the March 1582. The *ikki* then prepared for a long siege. Archaeological research at Torigoe has found large earthenware storage jars buried in the ground, and there is also evidence that, when the castle changed hands, considerable alterations were made to the defences in preparation for Nobunaga's counterattack. The forts were nevertheless taken and destroyed, and this time no chance of resurgence was to be allowed. Three hundred men of the *ikki* were crucified on the riverbed, and, after this gruesome local display, Sakuma Morimasa carried out further suppression with great severity.

One of the reconstructed gates of Torigoe castle, which changed hands several times before succumbing to Nobunaga's final operations against the Ikkō Ikki of Kaga.

By the year 1581, most of the Kinai area was in Nobunaga's hands, but, along with Saika, one very small province remained out of reach thanks to the tenacity of its *ikki*. That province was Iga, which had supported the Ōmi *ikki* in their earlier efforts against Nobunaga. Iga now became the site of the first and second Tenshō Iga no Ran (the Iga Rebellions of the

---

1   SKK 1965, pp.304–05.

Tenshō Era) of 1579 and 1581, although the title is somewhat misleading because Iga was defined as rebellious only by Oda Nobunaga. The first incursion into the province was carried out by his son Nobukatsu in 1579 and was a humiliating failure. The second was directed by Nobunaga himself in 1581 and crushed the Iga *ikki* by the application of overwhelming force.

Iga's resistance to Nobunaga went back to the time when Oda Nobukatsu had been adopted into the Kitabatake family of neighbouring Ise. When he succeeded to the family headship, the surviving members of the Kitabatake did not accept his succession meekly. Takigawa Kazumasu put down the rebellion with great severity, and many of the defeated Kitabatake samurai fled to Iga, which stayed remarkably defiant and fiercely independent. Nobunaga first entrusted the pacification of Iga to Nobukatsu, but the result was as embarrassing as the battle of Tedorigawa had been. The *ikki* were able to make preparations and assembled in three places from which any point of attack could be speedily reinforced. The first attack route was led by Oda Nobukatsu in person across the Pass of Nagano. In the poetic words of the local *gunkimono* called *Iran ki*, 'his gold umbrella standard came out of the black cloud of the thick morning fog from out of which he pushed forward, as wonderful as the rising of the sun.'9 Yet the Iga *ikki* were ready for him and attacked the Ise army in a classic ambush:

Oda Nobukatsu, whose disastrous invasion of Iga in 1579 brought retribution on his head from his father, Nobunaga.

> The Ise samurai were confused in the gloom and scattered in all directions. They fled but were cut down in the secluded valley or on the steep rocks. They chased them into the muddy rice fields and surrounded them ... Some killed each other by mistake. Others committed suicide and it is not known how many thousands were killed.2

The second division of Nobukatsu's army under Takigawa Kazumasu crossed by another mountain pass and suffered equally. Riding with them was Tsuge Saburōzaemon, the former senior retainer and alleged murderer

---

2  Momochi Orinosuke (ed.), *Kōsei Iran ki* (Iga-Ueno: Tekisui Shoin, 1897), Chapter 2, p.8.

of the late Kitabatake Tomonori of Ise, so the Iga *ikki* saw a chance for revenge.[11] The death of a senior retainer on the battlefield at the hands of an *ikki* was such a disgraceful occurrence that the killing of Tsuge receives a mention in *Shinchō-Kō ki*. In Nobunaga's supposed words castigating his son, the unspeakable death of Tsuge Saburōzaemon was the result of a serious error on Nobukatsu's part.[3]

Two years later, the Oda army returned over six different synchronised attack routes. This time, the strategy was directed by Nobunaga himself, although he did not make an appearance in Iga until after the victory was secured. A scorched-earth policy was put into operation by his ruthless and numerically superior army, with the overall aim being one of forcing the defenders to abandon their villages and take to fortified positions, thus reducing the opportunity for the guerrilla tactics that had worked so well in 1579. The *Shinchō-Kō ki* account shows how thorough Nobunaga's process was:

> All moved as one through the Sanagu hills of Iga province, and temples throughout the province were completely destroyed by fire from the Ichinomiya on down. The enemy responded by an ashigaru sally out of Sanagu castle. Takigawa Sakon and Hori Kyūtarō waited for their moment and charged in with their horses, killing more than ten of their finest samurai.[4]

Yet Nobunaga's army did not have it all their own way. They may have forced the Iga samurai into forts, but, once any siege became prolonged, the opportunity arose for the garrison to practise guerrilla techniques on the besiegers that would later form the basis of the legends of the Iga ninja, and there is a very good illustration of this in the account of the siege of Kashiwara:

> At night they slipped out in secret and raided the camps of all the generals and set fire to them using various techniques. Because of this the enemy became more careful and strengthened the guard. Everyone kept watch, because everyone knew what was going on, so they grew less careless. However, Niwa Nagahide's camp was attacked by night on several occasions, and night after night his guards were murdered. Over a hundred men were killed, and because of this the enemy were placed in fear and trembling. Their alertness decreased because they could not rest at all.[5]

---

3   SKK 1965, p.262.
4   SKK 1965, p.333.
5   KIK 1897, Chapter 7, pp.14–16.

Eventually, the Oda army triumphed, and Nobunaga went to Iga to see the tiny province that had caused him so much trouble. *Shinchō-Kō ki* diplomatically omits an attempt on Nobunaga's life that is supposed to have happened during his visit, because, as Nobunaga sat surrounded by his followers, guns were fired at him from three different directions. Although the shots missed Nobunaga, they succeeded in killing seven or eight of his retainers.[6] In spite of this, instead of carrying out a final punitive massacre, Nobunaga behaved with mercy towards the survivors, even if all their temples, shrines, castles and mansions were burned to the ground along with any historical records they may have contained. The *ikki* members who had not already fled to other provinces were quickly disarmed as the province passed rapidly under the new and unwelcome situation of daimyo control. Three out of Iga's four districts were assigned to the victorious Nobukatsu, and the remaining one was given to Nobunaga's brother Oda Nobukane (1548–1614).[7]

## The End of the Takeda

The pacification of Iga was destined to be Nobunaga's final victory over an *ikki*, but greater fish still remained to be hauled in, and the ongoing prospects for success were very good. Writing from Nagasaki on 15 February 1582, Father Gaspar Coelho summed up Nobunaga's achievements to date in the words 'Lord of these parts for many years now: Nobunaga, who with his effort, and wiles of a small kingdom that had in a short time made himself master of the entire monarchy of Japan, and now possesses thirty-four kingdoms'.[8] The new year promised to be another time of triumph when Nobunaga would break through three crucial barriers: the Takeda territories in Kai and Shinano, the Mōri domain of the Inland Sea and the Chōsokabe lands on Shikoku island. If he overcame all of them, Nobunaga would be unassailable, and, if Fróis is to be believed, Nobunaga may even have begun contemplating an invasion of China.[9]

He began with the Takeda. Their clan had been ruled by Shingen's heir, Takeda Katsuyori, since 1573, and it was a measure of how indecisive the battle of Nagashino had been that Takeda Katsuyori was still at large and conducting campaigns in the Kantō seven years later. Those operations lay far from Nobunaga's sphere of influence, being directed particularly against the Hōjō family. There was still no direct threat to Nobunaga early in 1582 when Nobunaga was informed that Kiso Yoshimasa, Katsuyori's brother-in-law and a key supporter, had declared for the Oda cause.[10] That was an

---

6 KIK 1897, Chapter 4, p.5.
7 SKK 1965, p.334.
8 *Cartas* 1598, vol. 2, f. 30r.
9 *Cartas* 1598, vol. 2, f. 63v.
10 SKK 1965, p.352.

opportunity to be grasped with both hands, so Nobunaga immediately ordered Nobutada to secure the border forts and take hostages to guarantee Kiso's new allegiance while he prepared to take the field himself. He drew up a plan of attack within a few days that brought in Tokugawa Ieyasu and Hōjō Ujimasa against the geographically vast Takeda domain. Nobunaga committed considerable resources to the operation, sparing only Hideyoshi and Akechi Mitsuhide, who were already engaged with the Mōri, his son Nobutaka, who was preparing for the Shikoku invasion, and a small contingent who were sitting in front of Kōyasan, whose warrior monks had been proving more than a little troublesome. Following the Araki revolt, they had given sanctuary to Murashige's defeated army and were now facing destruction similar to that inflicted upon Mount Hiei, a fate they would escape only because of Nobunaga's death.[11]

Katsuyori had established a new castle at Shinpu, an act that was regarded by his followers as a bad omen because his father, Takeda Shingen, had been content with a fortified mansion, relying on his loyal subjects to be all the walls he needed. In 1582, there was a radical change of heart among his supporters when some started betraying him. As *Shinchō-Kō ki* puts it in a long and remorseless account, 'high and low seized the moment to render loyal service to Nobunaga by joining forces with him'.[12] Of those who belonged the 'high', most of Katsuyori's closest retainers began abandoning the Takeda flag. Even the veteran Anayama Baisetsu, who had been one of Shingen's 'Twenty-Four Generals', left Katsuyori to his fate, and soon few outside his closest relatives were left. On hearing of Nobunaga's approach, Katsuyori withdrew into the mountains, but, when he took up an offer of a stronger refuge from Oyamada Nobushige, a general who had survived Nagashino, he would find the gates of Iwadono castle closed against him. Only the sons of Tsuchiya Masatsugu, who had been killed at Nagashino, stood beside Katsuyori to the last, and, while the Tsuchiya brothers held the enemy back, Katsuyori and his wife committed suicide on the battlefield of Tenmokuzan.

The attack on the Takeda by his generals and allies had carried all before it, so, by the time Nobunaga arrived on the scene, his advance into the mountains of Kai had become less of a military campaign and more of a royal progress, taking in some sightseeing along the way. He seems to have enjoyed seeing Mount Fuji for the first time in his life.[13] Katsuyori's suicide then left Nobunaga free to return in triumph and enjoy similarly luxurious travel, leaving Oda Nobutada in Kai to prove that he was the equal of his father in ruthlessness. For example, in his desire to punish the monks of the Erinji for hiding his enemies, Nobutada drove all its inhabitants into the upper storey of the temple's gatehouse. He then packed the stairwells with

---

11  Owada Tetsuo, 'Kōyasan yakiuchi', *Rekishi Dokuhon*, 33:19 (1988), pp.104–11.
12  SKK 1965, p.351.
13  SKK 1965, p.367.

# THE FINAL YEARS

straw and set it alight. Ōta Gyūichi admires the behaviour of the prelate Kaisen, who sat unflinching at prayer as he was burned to death.[14]

Nobunaga took over the Takeda's former provinces, which brought him perilously close to the Hōjō domain for the first time in their shared history. At first, suggestions were made for a marriage alliance with Nobunaga in return for the cession of territory, but that idea came to nothing because Nobunaga had his own ideas about how the former Takeda territories should be administered. In spite of protestations from the Hōjō, he gave the western half of Kōzuke and two districts of Shinano to the loyal Takigawa Kazumasu. There was peace in the Kantō as the Oda *tenka* reached its ultimate size.

## The End at Honnōji

After the fall of the Takeda, Nobunaga began serious preparations for a deeper penetration along the coast of the Inland Sea against the Mōri and for the operation against Shikoku. He was so confident of taking the island that he had already handed out its four provinces as rewards. With the Takeda defeated and the invasion poised to lift off, the mood at Azuchi castle was therefore one of celebration and anticipation, but, on 7 June 1582, the party was disrupted by the arrival of a messenger from Toyotomi Hideyoshi. He was currently laying siege to the Mōri possession of Takamatsu castle in Bitchū province by building a dam and earthworks to flood the place. The action had drawn out the main Mōri body to their assistance, and Hideyoshi had realised that this was a golden opportunity to crush them once and for all. Nobunaga was equally enthusiastic when the intelligence reached him. Faced by this gift from heaven, he decided to act swiftly and confront the Mōri in person, just as he had intended to do with the Takeda, and, as in their case, he sent certain captains on ahead.[15]

Nobunaga soon began to move westwards and was so carefree that he stayed the night of 19 June in the temple of Honnōji in Kyoto

Akechi Mitsuhide, whose dramatic betrayal of Nobunaga in 1582 led to the latter's death at the temple of Honnōji. Mitsuhide is shown here in an earlier and noble role as a loyal general.

---

14   SKK 1965, pp.367–68.
15   SKK 1965, p.381.

## ODA NOBUNAGA: SAMURAI COMMANDER 1534–82

with only a few attendants as company; the Horse Guards were apparently garrisoning Azuchi castle. His vanguard was led by Akechi Mitsuhide, whose own castle of Kameyama lay en route in Tanba province, but Mitsuhide's troops were in for a surprise, because he ordered them to turn around and march back to Kyoto, where Nobunaga apparently intended to inspect them. Mitsuhide commanded the soldiers to have their arms in readiness and the matches alight in their serpentines, reassuring them that, on entering Kyoto, he wanted to give Nobunaga a sight of the fine, well-drilled force he led.

At dawn, Mitsuhide and his 13,000 troops arrived back in Kyoto, but they were not to be lined up in dress order in front of their commander-in-chief, Oda Nobunaga, to be inspected. Mitsuhide, 'wondering if he could make himself master of the monarchy of Japan',[16] attacked Honnōji, where Nobunaga was sleeping. Taken completely by surprise at this failure of trust, Nobunaga first thought that a quarrel had broken out until a fusillade of gunfire made him realise that he was now in the position into which he had placed Imagawa Yoshimoto 22 years earlier. He had just got out of bed and had washed his face and hands when he received an arrow in the ribs.

The final attack on Nobunaga at Honnōji. After defending himself valiantly, Nobunaga retired to an inner room and committed suicide. (KMGF 1886)

---

16   *Cartas* 1598, vol. 2, f. 64v.

He drew it out, seized a *naginata* and laid about him vigorously until his arm was shattered by a harquebus ball. Realising that all was lost, the proud Oda Nobunaga withdrew to an inner room and committed suicide.

Akechi Mitsuhide then rushed to eliminate every other member of Nobunaga's family that he could find. Oda Nobutada had fled to the safety of Nijō castle but was defeated there and committed suicide. Oda Nobutaka, waiting in Sakai for the Shikoku invasion to go ahead, was deserted by his men and in his panic ordered the assassination of his cousin Oda Nobuzumi, whom he suspected of being involved in the Akechi plot. The evidence was wholly circumstantial: Nobuzumi was married to Akechi Mitsuhide's daughter, and his father, Nobuyuki, had long ago been murdered by Nobunaga, but that was enough to allow one of Nobunaga's sons to continue Akechi's work for him. Nobutaka could instead have taken the lead against the usurper, but his actions left the way open for Toyotomi Hideyoshi to become his father's avenger rather than anyone with the name of Oda, and Hideyoshi's response was swift. On receiving the news of Nobunaga's death, he patched up a truce with the Mōri and marched quickly back towards Kyoto, where he defeated and killed the usurper Akechi Mitsuhide at the battle of Yamazaki. Hideyoshi then outmanoeuvred Nobunaga's surviving sons by proclaiming Nobunaga's infant grandson as heir and himself as guardian. The *tenka* created by Nobunaga had virtually disappeared overnight, to be reclaimed and rebuilt by someone else within a very short space of time.

## Nobunaga's Legacy

Oda Nobunaga – one of the greatest and most controversial figures in Japanese history, the enemy of militant Buddhism and militant *ikki* alike – had perished, and his accomplishments had died with him. At the time of his death, he controlled 29 out of Japan's 66 provinces and parts of two others, almost one third of the entire land mass of contemporary Japan excluding Hokkaidō. Almost all were lost, with only the landholdings of his surviving sons left intact.

Among the many military achievements to be claimed for him in retrospect, the most important is that Nobunaga is commonly believed to have set the reunification of Japan in motion by utilising firearms in a unique and masterful manner. Looking at his struggles against Ishiyama Honganji and his experiences against gunfire at Tennōji and in Kii, it may be more accurate to think that Nobunaga's unification of the country was delayed by other people's guns. History would, however, construct a very different image of him, bending the reality of his achievements to make him into a brilliant Japanese innovator who had anticipated Europe's military revolution by an entire decade.

More realistically, we may regard Oda Nobunaga as the master of massacres and intimidation, the last of the opportunistic and ruthless *sengoku daimyō*. He then became the first of the 'super-daimyo' who would

## ODA NOBUNAGA: SAMURAI COMMANDER 1534–82

eventually unite Japan under one sword, a transformation that required all the skills that Nobunaga undoubtedly possessed. Among those was an eye for long-term strategy, and, through his settlement of provinces and elimination of opponents, he set a trend that Hideyoshi and Ieyasu would follow successfully. In that, the popular contrast that depicts Nobunaga as a savage and the other unifiers as geniuses is rendered invalid, because several of their more peaceful techniques such as sword hunts had already been anticipated by Nobunaga.[17] On the battlefield, he had always been brave and calculating, failing only to secure decisive victories at Anegawa and Nagashino owing to a cautious approach that must have looked sensible at the time. He also demonstrated throughout the vital necessity of building up a loyal and talented warrior band to whom he could safely delegate coterminous campaigns. Through that systematic approach to his senior ranks alone, Oda Nobunaga proved to be a great samurai commander, only to be betrayed by the system at the very last moment.

Seizing a *naginata*, Suzuki Magoroku dances on his one good leg to celebrate the death of Nobunaga. (KMGF 1886)

---

17  Elison and Smith (eds), *Warlords*, p.68.

I will finish with a little anecdote that neatly encapsulates the reaction to Nobunaga's death among his longest-lasting enemies. When the Honnōji Incident happened, Niwa Nagahide (1535–1585) was busy conducting a siege on Nobunaga's behalf of Saginomori Gobō, the replacement Honganji in Kii province. After a fierce battle across the temple walls, the defenders were waiting for the morrow and what they anticipated would be their certain defeat when a messenger arrived with the news of Nobunaga's death. The besiegers, who had yet to be informed of the tragedy by their own envoy, were stunned at the noise of a celebration coming from within the temple. Among those rejoicing was Suzuki Magoroku, who commanded a unit of Saika's mercenary harquebusiers. During the fighting of the day before, he had been shot in the leg and had to be carried to safety. Now, with the enemy having lost their great commander, Magoroku seized a *naginata* and performed a dance of victory on his one good leg to celebrate the death of Oda Nobunaga, the enemy of Buddhism and *ikki* alike, the man who was supposed to have outgunned them and the perpetrator of massacres.

Suzuki Magoroku no doubt felt that the Honganji should be given some credit for the achievement, and it is more than likely that the Jesuit missionaries would have agreed with him. In a letter to his superiors on 15 February 1582, Father Gaspar Coelho had already expressed an opinion about Nobunaga that 'if the monks had not been around he would already have become master of all Japan'.[18] Within six months of that letter being written, Nobunaga, the master of massacres – if not of muskets – and the man who had dominated the world of Japan that the missionaries had entered, was no more.

The mausoleum of Oda Nobunaga on the holy mountain of Kōyasan. Ironically, Kōyasan only escaped destruction comparable to that inflicted upon Mount Hiei because of Nobunaga's death.

---

18   *Cartas* 1598, vol. 2, f. 30r.

# Colour Plates Commentary

**Plate A.** Oda Nobunaga at the head of his army c. 1573. He is accompanied by the two leaders of his Horse Guards: Maeda Toshiie of the red *horo* unit and Sassa Narimasa of the black *horo* unit, so named from their *horo* (ornamental cloaks). His flags bear his favourite design of the coin motif and have small pennants with the motto of the Nichiren Sect. Nobunaga's helmet and golden umbrella are proudly displayed to show his presence on the battlefield, where a discarded flag of the Asakura family bears witness to a recent victory. (Original artwork for this book by Emmanuel Valerio)

**Plate B.** A life-sized diorama formerly on display at Kiyosu castle, showing Oda Nobunaga performing a chant from the Noh play *Atsumori* before setting off for the battle of Okehazama in 1560.

**Plate C.** The death of Imagawa Yoshimoto at the battle of Okehazama. In contrast to the effete image traditionally claimed for him, Yoshimoto fought bravely before being overcome.

**Plate D.** The army of Asakura Yoshikage enter the river at the battle of Anegawa in 1570. This is a modern painted screen done in traditional style on display at Nagahama Castle Museum.

**Plate E.** Endō Naotsugu infiltrates Nobunaga's inner circle of Horse Guards at the battle of Anegawa but is rapidly overcome before getting anywhere near his target.

**Plate F.** Modern Gifu City, which Nobunaga made into his headquarters, proudly displays this golden statue of him with details that emphasise Nobunaga's European connections: a harquebus, a European breastplate and helmet and a cloak.

**Plate G.** An armour of *dō-maru* style, typical of the later years of Oda Nobunaga. (ColBase: Integrated Collections Database of the National Institute for Cultural Heritage, Japan)

# COLOUR PLATES COMMENTARY

**Plate H.** The hero Mori Yoshinari (1523–1570), who lifted the dying Oda Nobuharu on to his shoulders before being killed himself in a battle at Sakamoto in 1570.

**Plate I.** The restored outer gateway of the Asakura mansion of Ichijōdani, destroyed by Nobunaga in 1573.

**Plate J.** A modern interpretation of the banner showing the crucified Torii Sune'emon, which a retainer of the Takeda had made in admiration of his bravery at Nagashino. This is from the annual Nagashino Battle Festival.

**Plate K.** This is claimed to be the actual helmet worn by Nobunaga at the battle of Nagashino. It is on display at the privately owned Kawagoe Historical Museum.

**Plate L.** Oda Nobunaga at the battle of Nagashino in 1575, showing his *nobori* banners with the coin motif and the Nichiren pennants. His helmet is carried in state. From a copy of the original Nagashino Screen in Nakatsu Castle Museum.

**Plate M.** The battle of Nagashino, showing the Takeda troops being mown down by gunfire in the traditional interpretation of the famous battle. From a copy of the original Nagashino Screen in Nakatsu Castle Museum.

**Plate N.** A fine modern interpretation in traditional style at Azuchi Castle Museum of Nobunaga's multi-storeyed masterpiece of Azuchi castle.

**Plate O.** Akechi Mitsuhide, whose treachery brought about the death of Nobunaga at the Honnōji in 1582. This painting of him hangs in his restored castle of Kameyama, where Mitsuhide is uniquely honoured.

**Plate P.** This armour is said to have belonged to Akechi Mitsuharu, a senior vassal of Akechi Mitsuhide. It is a valuable early example of the European-style Japanese armour. The rabbit's ears on the helmet express a desire for speed and agility. (ColBase: Integrated Collections Database of the National Institute for Cultural Heritage, Japan)

**Plate Q.** Oda (Kanbe) Nobutaka (1568–1583), Nobunaga's third son, who was preparing for the invasion of Shikoku island when Nobunaga died.

**Plate R.** Oda Nobunaga, the first of Japan's unifiers, from a hanging scroll owned by Himeji Castle Museum.

# Bibliography

## Illustrated Books

Several of the pictures used here have been taken from illustrated books of the Edo and Meiji Periods that cover the life and career of Oda Nobunaga. *Ehon Shūi Shinchō ki* was published in 1803. *Ehon Ishiyama Gunki* went into numerous popular editions using moveable type, including one with only pictures and no text. The war tale *Ishiyama Gunki*, written originally in about 1718, also exists in later illustrated versions. *Ehon Taikō ki* of 1799 and *Ehon Toyotomi kunkō ki* of 1855 also appear here, and the 1886 edition of *Kaisei Mikawa Gofudo ki* also includes a few very good pictures. Where I use double-page spreads, I have spliced the two pages together to reconstruct the artist's original picture as fully as possible. Otherwise, particular details have been selected and are noted. The abbreviations used in the captions are as follows:

EIG 1881: *Ehon Ishiyama Gunki* (woodblock printed edition)
EIG 1888: *Ehon Ishiyama Gunki* (pictures only edition)
EIG 1891: *Ehon Ishiyama Gunki* (moveable type edition)
ESSK 1803: *Ehon Shūi Shinchō ki*
ETK 1799: *Ehon Taikō ki*
ETKK 1855: *Ehon Toyotomi kunkō ki*
IG 1895: *Ishiyama Gunki*
KMGF 1886: *Kaisei Mikawa Gofudo ki*.

## Primary Sources

*Cartas* 1598, vol. 1: Anon., *Cartas que os padres e irmãos da Companhia de Iesus escreuerão dos Reynos de Iapão & China aos da mesma Companhia da India, & Europa des do Anno de 1549 até o de 1580* (Em Euora: Manoel de Lyra, 1598)
*Cartas* 1598, vol. 2: Anon., *Segunda parte das cartas de Iapão que escreuerão os padres, & irmãos da companhia de Iesus* (Em Euora: Manoel de Lyra, 1598)

ESSK 1803: Niwa, Tōkei, and Ryūkōsai, Nyokei, *Ehon Shūi Shinchō ki* (Tokyo: Publisher unknown, 1803), vol. 5
IG 1895: Okamoto, Sensuke (ed.), *Ishiyama Gunki* (Tokyo: Igyō-kan, 1895)
KIK 1897: Momochi, Orinosuke (ed.), *Kōsei Iran ki* (Iga-Ueno: Tekisui Shoin, 1897)
KMGF 1886: Narushima, Motonao (ed.), *Kaisei Mikawa Gofudo ki* (Tokyo: Kinshōdō, 1886), vol. 1
KMGF 1976: Kuwata, Tadachika, and Utagawa, Terao (eds), *Kaisei Mikawa Gofudo ki* (Tokyo: Akita Shoten, 1976), vols 1–2
SKK 1965: Kuwata, Tadachika (ed.), *Shinchō-Kō ki* (Tokyo: Jinbutsu Ōraisha, 1965)
Yuasa, Jōzan, *Jōzan Kidan* (Tokyo: Yohodo, 1912), <https://archive.org/details/jozankidan00yuasuoft/page/766/mode/2up>, p.88, accessed 31 May 2024

## Primary Sources in Translation

CLN 2011: Elisonas, J. S. A., and Lamers, J. P. (trans and eds), *The Chronicle of Lord Nobunaga by Ōta Gyūichi* (Leiden: Brill, 2011)

## Secondary Sources

Elison, George, and Smith, Bardwell L. (eds), *Warlords, Artists and Commoners: Japan in the Sixteenth Century* (Honolulu: University of Hawaii Press, 1981)
Enya, Kikumi, *Ishiyama kassen wo yomi naosu* (Tokyo: Hōzōkan, 2021)
Fujii, Hisao, *Dokyumento Sengoku Jō* (Tokyo: Kawade Shobo Shinsha, 1965)
Inufuku, Chihuahua, 'Tennōji no tatakai', *Sengoku History* (2019), <https://sengoku-his.com/13>, accessed 8 March 2025
Katsura, Hidezumi, 'Ishiyama Honganji Kassen', *Rekishi Dokuhon*, 33:19 (1988), pp.96–103
Lamers, Jeroen, *Japonius Tyrannus: The Japanese Warlord Oda Nobunaga Reconsidered* (Leiden: Hotei, 2000)
Lidin, Olof G., *Tanegashima: The Arrival of Europe in Japan* (Copenhagen: Nias Press, 2002)
McMullin, Neil, *Buddhism and the State in Sixteenth-Century Japan* (Princeton: Princeton University Press, 1984)
Okuno, Takahiro, *Ashikaga Yoshiaki* (Tokyo: Yoshikawa Kōbunkan, 1960)
Owada, Tetsuo, *Hideyoshi no tenka tōitsu sensō* (Tokyo: Yoshikawa Kobunkan, 2006)
Owada, Tetsuo, 'Kōyasan yakiuchi', *Rekishi Dokuhon*, 33:19 (1988), pp.104–11
Pitelka, Morgan, *Reading Medieval Ruins: Urban Life and Destruction in Sixteenth-Century Japan* (Cambridge: Cambridge University Press, 2022)

Sadler, A. L., *The Maker of Modern Japan: The Life of Tokugawa Ieyasu* (London: Allen and Unwin, 1937)

Sansom, George, *A History of Japan, 1334-1615* (London: Cresset Press, 1961)

Shapinsky, Peter D., *Lords of the Sea: Pirates, Violence and Commerce in Late Medieval Japan* (Ann Arbor: University of Michigan Press, 2014)

Suzuki, Masaya, *Katana to kubotori* (Tokyo: Heibonsha, 2000)

Suzuki, Masaya, *Sengoku teppō: Yōhei-tai tenkabito ni sakaratta Kishū Saiga shū* (Tokyo: Heibonsha, 2004)

Suzuki, Masaya, *Teppō to Nihonjin* (Tokyo: Chikuma Shobō, 2000)

Takahashi, Kenichi, *Hata Sashimono* (Tokyo: Akita Shoten, 1965)

Turnbull, Stephen, 'Biting the Bullet: A Reassessment of the Development, Use and Impact of Early Firearms in Japan', *Vulcan*, 8 (2020), pp.26–53

Turnbull, Stephen, *Hōjō: Samurai Warlords 1487-1590* (Warwick: Helion and Company, 2023)

Turnbull, Stephen, *The Ōnin War 1467-77: A Turning Point in Samurai History* (Warwick: Helion and Company, 2021)

Udagawa, Takehisa (ed.), *Rekishi no naka no teppō denrai, Tanegashima kara Boshin sensō made* (Sakura City: Kokuritsu Rekishi Monzoku Hakubutsukan, 2006)

Udagawa, Takehisa, *Shinsetsu Teppō denrai* (Tokyo: Heibonsha, 2006)

Udagawa, Takehisa, *Teppō denrai: heiki ga kataru kinsei no tanjō* (Tōkyō: Kōdansha, 2013)

Varshavskaya, Elena, *Heroes of the Grand Pacification* (Amsterdam: Hotei Publishing, 2005)

# About the author

Stephen Turnbull took his first degree at Cambridge and has two MAs (in Theology and Military History). In 1996 he received a PhD from Leeds University for his thesis on Japan's Kakure Kirishitan which won the Japan Festival Literary Award in 1998. Having lectured in East Asian Studies and Theology he is now retired and is an Honorary Lecturer at Leeds, a Research Associate at SOAS and Visiting Professor of Japanese Studies at Akita International University. His expertise has helped with numerous projects including films, television and the award-winning strategy game Shogun Total War. *Oda Nobunaga: Samurai Commander 1534-82* is his fifth book in the series "From Retinue to Regiment".

# Other titles in the From Retinue to Regiment series:

No 1 *Richard III and the Battle of Bosworth* Mike Ingram

No 2 *Tanaka 1587: Japan's Greatest Unknown Samurai Battle* Stephen Turnbull

No 3 *The Army of the Swabian League 1525* Doug Miller

No 4 *The Italian Wars Volume 1: The Expedition of Charles VIII into Italy and the Battle of Fornovo* Massimo Predonzani & Alberici Vincenzo, translated by Irene Maccolini

No 5 *The Commotion Time: Tudor Rebellion in the West, 1549* E.T. Fox

No 6 *The Italian Wars Volume 2: Agnadello 1509, Ravenna 1512, Marignano 1515* Massimo Predonzani & Alberici Vincenzo, translated by Rachele Tiso

No 7 *The Tudor Arte of Warre Volume 1: The Conduct of War from Henry VII to Mary I, 1485-1558* Jonathan Davies

No 8 *The Ethiopian-Adal War 1529-1543: The Conquest of Abyssinia* Jeffrey M. Shaw

No 9 *The Ōnin War: A Turning Point in Samurai History* Stephen Turnbull

No 10 *One Faith, One Law, One King: French Armies of the Wars of Religion 1562–1598* T J O'Brien de Clare

No 11 *The Italian Wars Volume 3: Francis I and the Battle of Pavia 1525* Massimo Predonzani & Alberici Vincenzo

No 12 *On the Borderlands of Great Empires: Transylvanian Armies 1541-1613* Florin Nicolae Ardelean

No 14 *The Art of Shooting Great Ordnance: A History of the Development, Manufacture and Use of Artillery, 1494–1628* Jonathan Davies

No 15 *The Italian Wars Volume 4: The Battle of Ceresole 1544 - The Crushing Defeat of the Imperial Army* Massimo Predonzani & Simon Miller

No 16 *The Men of Warre: The Clothes, Weapons and Accoutrements of the Scots at War 1460–1600* Jenn Scott

No 17 *The German Peasants' War 1524–26* Douglas Miller

No 18 *The Tudor Arte of Warre Volume 2: The conduct of war in the reign of Elizabeth I, 1558–1603: Diplomacy, Strategy, Campaigns and Battles* Jonathan Davies

No 19 *The Kalmar War 1611–1613: Gustavus Adolphus's First War* Michael Fredholm von Essen

No 20 *Hojo: Samurai Warlords 1487–1590* Stephen Turnbull

No 21 *The Battle of Castillon 1453: The Death Knell for English France* Peter Hoskins

No 22 *The Tudor Arte of Warre Volume 3: The Conduct of War in the Reign of Elizabeth I 1558-1603: The Elizabethan Army* Jonathan Davies

No 23 *Sweden's War in Muscovy 1609-1617: The Relief of Moscow and Conquest of Novgorod* Michael Fredholm von Essen

No 24 *'Of Kerns and Gallowglasses': Irish Armies of the Sixteenth Century, 1487-1587* Robert Gresh

No 25 *'The Italian Wars Volume 5: The Franco-Spanish War in Southern Italy 1502-1504* Massimo Predonzani

No 26 *The Sieges of Rhodes 1480 and 1522* Jonathan Davies

No 27 *The Swabian War of 1499: The first confrontation between Landsknechts and the Swiss* Albert Winkler

No 28 *'A Mighty Fortress of God': The Siege of Münster 1534-35* Doug Miller

No 29 *The Nine Years War 1593-1603 Part 1: The ascendancy of Irish arms and the road to Yellow Ford, 1593-1598* James O'Neil

No 30 *Elephants and Gunpowder: Southeast Asian Warfare 1380-1700* Stephen Turnbull

No 31 *The English Longbow - Investigating a Myth Volume 1: Performance and employment 1298-1485* Jonathan Davies

No 32 *The War of the Roses Volume 1: The Triumph of York 1455* David Grummitt

No 33 *The Battle of Pavia 1525: From the Chronicles and Tapestries of the Capodimonte* Massimo Predonzani

No 34 *Oda Nobunaga: Samurai Commander 1534-82* Stephen Turnbull